Caviar, Truffles, and Foie Gras

Caviar, Truffles, and Foie Gras

RECIPES FOR DIVINE INDULGENCE

BY KATHERINE ALFORD

Photographs by Ellen Silverman

CHRONICLE BOOKS
SAN FRANCISCO

TO ROBERT AND ABIGAIL, WHO MAKE LIFE LUXURIOUS.

Acknowledgments

I am indebted to Alice Martel, my wonderfully supportive agent, for the idea for this book, which grew from a conversation we had when I was 8 months pregnant. It stayed only an idea, until 2 years later, when it was resurrected by the most encouraging editor anyone could hope for, Bill LeBlond. Since then, Bill has become a true friend and reassured me throughout the roller coaster ride of writing this book.

This book came about because of the generosity of all the people who work with these special foods every day. They took the time to answer my questions, share their expertise, and initiate me into the fascinating world of caviar, foie gras, and truffles. I am thoroughly grateful to George Faison of D'artagnan, Izzy Yanay of Hudson Valley Foie Gras, Eve Vega of Petrossian, Scott Skye of Caviar Russe, Mats and Daphne Engstrom of Tsar Nicoulai Caviar, Mark Grobman of Browne Trading, Rachel Collins at Carolyn Collins Caviar, Massimo Vidoni of Bosco Vivo, and Anne Zabar. A special thanks to Rosario Safina, who opened the door to the world of Italian truffles, and the very special Olga Urbani and Gianmaria Bonino, who made me welcome there. Along the way I was assisted by Samantha Fremont-Smith, who cheerfully trekked, shopped, tested, translated, and surfed the net for this book. She was a blessing. Very special thanks to Ellen Silverman for her beautiful photographs, and my dear friend Paul Grimes for his food styling.

I am humbled by my friends and family who put up with me during this time. I became a recluse in my kitchen and office and am thankful to find that they were still there when I emerged. Heartfelt thanks to Amy Treadwell and all the folks at Chronicle Books, who worked so hard to bring all the elements of this book together. Special thanks to my mother, Carolyn Coursen; Lyn and Harry Cason; Cathy Young; Bianca Henry; Naomi Horisford; David Sternbach and Erin Cramer; Roy Moscovitz and Anne Edelstein and their children Eva and Eli; who encouraged, tasted, and inspired. Thank you to my daughter Abigail, who continued to shine while I worked too much. This book would never have been, without the unwavering support of my husband, Robert Johnson. His love is my foundation.

Permissions
P. 9: Excerpt from *Fly Truffle* by Gustaf Sobin. Copyright © 2000 by W.W. Norton & Company. Reprinted by permission.

P. 87: Excerpt from *Speak, Memory: An Autobiography Revisited* by Vladimir Vladimirovich Nabokov. Copyright © 1989 by Everymans Library. Reprinted by permission.

P. 121: Excerpt from "Truffles" from *Earthly Paradise: An Autobiography* by Collette, edited by Robert Phelps. Translation copyright © 1966, renewed 1994 by Farrar, Straus & Giroux, Inc. Reprinted by permission of Farrar, Straus & Giroux, LLC.

Library of Congress Cataloging-in-Publication Data available.

ISBN 0-8118-2791-7
Printed in China

Prop styling by Betty Alfenito
Food styling by Paul Grimes
Designed by Lori Barra, TonBo designs
Assisted by Sandra Koenig and Sarah Eisler
Production by Jan Marti, Command Z
Hand Lettering by Tim Hanrahan
Typeset in Sabon and Bell Gothic

Distributed in Canada by Raincoast Books
9050 Shaughnessy Street
Vancouver, BC V6P 6E5

10 9 8 7 6 5 4 3 2 1

Chronicle Books LLC
85 Second Street
San Francisco, California 94105

www.chroniclebooks.com

CONTENTS

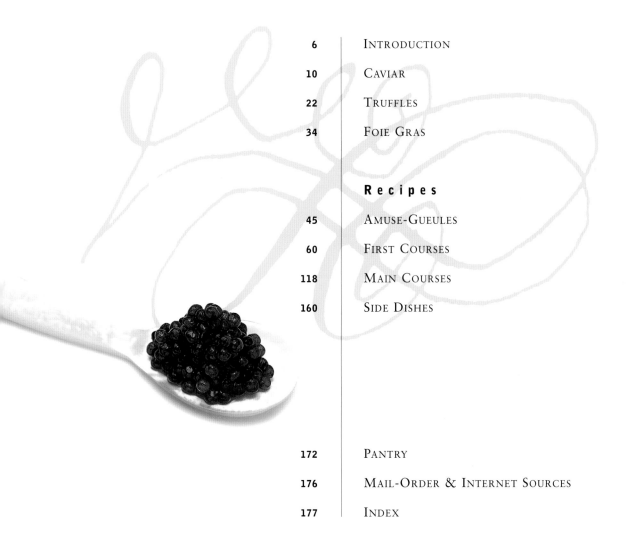

INTRODUCTION

No foods possess quite the same mystique as caviar, truffles, and foie gras. The pristine service of Caspian beluga caviar defines elegance. Showering a dish of fresh pasta with white Piedmont truffles turns the simple and familiar into something sublimely luxurious, and one of the ultimate pleasures of the table is the perfect marriage of the velvety rich foie gras with a noble Sauternes. Whether due to their unparalleled taste, scarcity, or whopping price, these foods cannot be eaten casually; they cause us to pause, take note, and celebrate. They transform us.

These delicacies are becoming ever more popular and familiar. Chefs across the country are featuring truffles on their menus in both traditional and innovative preparations. Foie gras is served in top restaurants seared, grilled, with pasta, in terrines, or as a final flourish in sauces—proving it's no chopped liver. Caviar, an icon of indulgence and jubilation, has never gone out of style. Caviar and other roes are used by knowing chefs as the ultimate garnish to a variety of dishes, from steak tartare to pasta.

Until recently in this country, these foods were relegated to the domain of restaurants, but America's burgeoning appetite for fine food has changed all that. Today the accessibility of these ingredients has greatly increased. Fancy food halls across the country display Russian caviar as well as a number of improved domestic varieties. Foie gras enthusiasts can choose from a wealth of products, fresh and prepared, including mousses, pâtés, whole lobes, and sliced medallions ready for searing. American truffle lovers can indulge their taste for truffles at supermarkets, with fresh truffles, seasoned oils, butters, and pastas. The Internet gives anyone access to fresh Hudson Valley foie gras, Oregon or Perigord truffles, and caviar from Mississippi sturgeon, Japanese flying fish, or Iranian Caspian beluga.

Americans savvy to the pleasure of the kitchen are taking these luxuries home. There is an undeniable thrill to preparing these foods in the

comfort of your own kitchen. To sensuously spoon caviar onto a fresh, warm homemade crepe or to prepare a meal enveloped by the heady aroma of a singular truffle—these are things home chefs dream about. It may seem ironic to talk about economy when discussing these foods, but there is a real savings to buying and serving these delicacies at home instead of paying top restaurant prices. I hope this book will be the guide to give you the confidence to cook with these exciting ingredients.

Working on this book has been an obvious pleasure. My experience with these ingredients began over fifteen years ago, as the executive sous-chef at the Quilted Giraffe, a four-star New York restaurant. During my tenure, I was responsible for the purchasing and receiving of truffles, foie gras, and caviar, as well as for the quality control and handling and cooking of these products. I oversaw the restaurant's active truffle concession, cooked a truckload of foie gras, and handled hundreds of original tins of Caspian caviar. Although I had worked with these ingredients, one of the surprises of writing this book was how different it was living with caviar, foie gras, and truffles.

What most people know about these foods is that they are expensive, but that is a small part of their story. Primordial caviar, the ultimate symbol of indulgence and fecundity, is the source of more intrigue than the best crime novel. Black-market deals, guns, and smuggling are as much a part of caviar's identity as ascot-clad gentlemen and Champagne. Caviar is always a surprise, with each batch of the dark eggs layered with a unique, complex flavor. My enjoyment of caviar moves me to examine the real issues of how we sustain this unique food while protecting the sturgeon and the environment at the same time.

Truffles are thrilling, magical, perfuming the kitchen with a dense aroma like the deep, natural breath of the earth. They are exotic and uncompromisingly wild, almost gamey—unexpected in a vegetable. Sharing them at the table is always a heightened pleasure. Writers like Colette, Dumas, and Brillat-Savarin have spoken of their power on the senses, either as an aphrodisiac or as a muse. I found that eating truffles, although not considered hallucinogenic, have a profound impact on my dreams, which become more vivid, focused, and incredibly lucid. Gustaf Sobin in his novel *The Fly-Truffler* describes this phenomenon beautifully.

. . . the truffle affected one's awakened body, one's conscious thoughts. It reassured the senses with its warm, earthy aroma, placed one's entire being in a raised state of receptivity. It didn't provoke the dream so much as create the conditions . . . in which the dream might occur.

Foie gras is an awesome product, the swollen liver of a duck or a goose, made in a strange partnership between humans and nature. Rich and divinely indulgent, foie gras engenders a passionate debate about animal rights as well as national loyalties to American and French products. I think of caloric and controversial foie gras as the Eartha Kitt of the food world: What makes it so good is that it is a little bit bad. A small amount of it will transform a simple dish into something extraordinary, whether a pot of beans, a bowl of figs, or a chicken stew.

Having these ingredients in your kitchen can give you a renewed pleasure in the ritual of cooking. They deserve a special respect and should be prepared in dishes without shortcuts or compromised flavors. That doesn't mean that you need a battery of cooks to enjoy these foods, quite the contrary. Due to their distinctive qualities and tastes, they don't need overwrought recipes to make them shine, which makes them perfect for home cooks. The recipes in this book use straightforward techniques and accessible combinations of foods. So enjoy the process, turn on some great music, and savor the luxury of cooking with these wonderful foods.

CAVIAR

Caviar is a phenomenon: exotic, scarce, mysterious, an event. As *the* symbol of luxury, the small, delicate eggs of the sturgeon capture our imagination. Few foods have such an aura. Whether as a food lover's rite of passage, a benchmark of personal success, or a once-in-a-lifetime experience, consuming caviar always makes an event seem larger than life. For some, when the little black pearls burst on the roof of the mouth, they become a symbol for all the things we define as grand, chic, or powerful. Without a doubt, part of caviar's charm is its lush image, but if that were the sum of its parts, this delicacy would not withstand the whims of fashion. At the foundation of caviar's prestigious reputation is the fact that it truly is an extraordinary food.

CAVIAR'S HISTORY

The word *caviar* comes from the Turkish *khavyar*, and refers to the salted unfertilized eggs of the sturgeon. Sturgeon, members of the family Acipenseridae, are found only in the Northern Hemisphere and are an impressive clan of fish. Some are giant, all are gentle. These toothless, cartilaginous fish have prehistoric origins, and they look the part. Instead of scales, they are covered with rows of bony plates called scutes. Most species are marine fish that return to freshwater rivers to spawn, and unlike salmon, which expire after releasing their eggs, they live to spawn again.

Humans have feasted on sturgeon for its meaty flesh and eggs since ancient times. Curing foods with salt is a basic preservation technique used with many foods; there are bas-reliefs in Egypt that depict fishermen curing fish roe with salt. Sturgeon has long been prized throughout the Eastern Mediterranean. Carthaginian coins minted around 600 B.C. depict a

sturgeon. Aristotle wrote of the fish in the fourth century B.C., and the poet Ovid called the fish "noble." Romans served the aristocratic fish at feasts, honoring them with a flourish of trumpets and adorning them with garlands. The sturgeon was fished not just for its flesh, which has a texture like veal, or for its roe, but also for its swim bladder, the source of isinglass, a gelatinous substance used to clarify wine.

RUSSIAN ROOTS

Although European caviar consumption fell off during the Middle Ages, nowhere was the fish more appreciated than in its native Russia. The deep Russian connection to the sturgeon can be linked to a vast supply in the Caspian and other Russian rivers, as well as to Russian conversion to Christianity in the tenth century. With the embracing of Orthodox practices came newly restricted foodways. Religious customs included long periods of fasting and prohibitions against meat, which fostered an appreciation for the local sturgeon and its roe. Religious instructions from 1280 prescribed: "For the fasting weeks, one should consume insipid food, rye kvass, and granular caviar." Caviar consumption, however, was not limited to the austere days of religious abstinence, and it was a regular feature at the Czar's table. Starting in 1675, Russian caviar was exported under the exclusive authority of the Czar.

Sturgeon were once plentiful in the rivers of Europe, swimming in the Gironde and Seine in France, the Po in Italy, the Elbe in Germany, and even in the Thames of England. In 1307, King Edward of England decreed that he owned any sturgeon landed in his kingdom. Although it was thought of as a particularly Russian specialty, caviar had regained status as a luxury food at elite tables by the seventeenth century. The Italians in particular adored it, serving it with vinegar and onions on grilled bread. Napoleon served French sturgeon, with the same pomp and flourish as the Romans. Unfortunately, by the end of the nineteenth century the fish fell victim to overfishing and industrial pollution in European waters. Today, it is rare to find sturgeon in any European rivers except in the Gironde estuary, where farm-raising efforts are in full swing.

CAVIAR IN THE UNITED STATES

The American story is sadly similar. Europeans found North American rivers—the Hudson, Delaware, and Kennebec in the east and the major rivers of the Northwest—teeming with sturgeon. In the late nineteenth century, a salty American caviar was served in New York bars, like peanuts, to stimulate beer and whiskey consumption, and Hudson River sturgeon was sold cheaply as "Albany beef." On the Columbia River in Oregon, horses were used to drag twelve-foot-long fish from the river, and there are stories of boats full of men being dragged under by a single fish. The 1800s saw a "caviar rush" on the eastern rivers and massive landings of sturgeon in the West. Although caviar was not popular with Americans, it was a significant lucrative export to Europe, particularly Germany. In 1895 and 1896, American caviar exports to Germany rivaled or exceeded the Russian caviar trade to that country. The drive to harvest sturgeon devastated stocks in a staggeringly short time, and by the beginning of the twentieth century the sturgeon fisheries on the Delaware and Hudson and in the Northwest collapsed. Today, sturgeon is no longer a commercial fish in the United States and can only be fished for sport.

STURGEON SPECIES

Of the twenty-seven species of sturgeon found in the world, four are main players in elite caviar circles. By legal definition, fish roe can only be labeled caviar (without being qualified, as in the case of salmon or lumpfish caviar) if from a sturgeon. The most significant of these are the beluga (*Huso huso*); the Russian sturgeon, also known as the osetra (*Acipenser gueldenstaedti*); the sevruga (*A. stellatas*); and the ship (*A. nudiventris*); all from the Caspian Sea. Each one of these species of fish is distinct and produces roe with particular qualities. Top-grade caviars are harvested from other sturgeon species, including the Chinese kaluga (*Huso dauricus*) and the American paddlefish (*Polyodontidae*), a sturgeon cousin.

Other fish are also appreciated for their roe, including salmon, whitefish, cod, flying fish, lumpfish, and trout. Although these roes are not substitutes for true caviar, they are wonderful products and provide an affordable alternative. Generally, fine sturgeon caviar should be savored au naturel, without any distracting garnish. Other roes, by contrast, offer the cook more creative options, since they can be successfully combined with other foods to add texture and bursts of flavor.

The beluga and freshwater kaluga are behemoths that can live for one hundred years, growing to more than sixteen feet long and over one thousand pounds, with fully mature fish weighing up to a ton. Beluga are found primarily in the Caspian, with smaller catches in the Black Sea, Azov, Danube, and eastern Mediterranean. Kaluga are found in the Amur River basin, which borders on Russia and China. The female, larger than the male, matures at twelve to eighteen years of age. When the females spawn in the spring and fall, the eggs can be 25 percent of the fish's total body weight. Beluga and kaluga caviar ranges in color from grayish to black, and the beads are the largest of all caviars, 2.5 to 3 millimeters in diameter. World-class beluga caviar is like butter: smooth, rich, and delicate. Although beluga is the nonplus ultra of caviar, its taste is the most ephemeral of the Caspian roes. The two decades it takes for this fish to reach adulthood contributes to beluga's rarity and highest price.

Russian sturgeon, or osetra, is found in the basin of the Caspian, Azov, and Black Seas. This fish matures at ten to twelve years and is seven feet long. Its eggs, smaller than those of the beluga, are 1.5 to 3 millimeters in diameter, with colors running the gamut from blackish to golden to even a greenish tint. It is the most important of the commercial sturgeons, and much of its stock in the Caspian comes from artificial propagation. Osetra has a nutty, fruity complexity reminiscent of the best extra-virgin olive oil. Because of its complex flavor, it is the caviar of choice for many connoisseurs (including the suave spy, James Bond).

Sevruga is the smallest of the commercially caught sturgeon, at about five feet long and sixty pounds in weight. It is a strangely beautiful fish, with starlike boney scales that run its length. It is the youngest of the mature fish and will produce eggs after seven years. Its eggs are also the smallest, about 1.2 to 2.5 millimeters in diameter. The flavor of sevruga is the boldest of all the Caspian caviars. When the tiny sevruga eggs pop in your mouth, it is as refreshing as a sea breeze. Some experts feel that because these eggs are so small, they absorb more salt in curing, contributing to their intense flavor. Because of sevruga's depth of flavor, it is the caviar to choose when making dishes with more layers of flavor, like beggar's purses, since it can hold its own combined with other foods. Ship (*A. nudiventris*), another fast-growing fish, produces a caviar similar to both osetra and sevruga and is sold under either one of those labels, depending on the size and color of its eggs.

CAVIAR TODAY

Ironically, the sturgeon, a creature that has been able to survive since prehistoric times, is highly vulnerable to the political and economic changes in the region. The upheaval that followed the breakup of the Soviet Union put the sturgeon fishery in turmoil. Caviar is a precious commodity representing substantial revenue, with worldwide retail sales estimated at $500 million. Beside the obvious economic incentive (much of the trade is in dollars), sturgeon is a basic foodstuff for the people of this area. An easy fish to catch, it spawns in shallow waters and is relatively docile. These factors have contributed to a mobocracy in the fishing communities, which were once tightly controlled by the Soviet system. Caviar became a lucrative prize, traded on the black market like drugs, and poachers, smuggling, bribery, illegal dealings, and serious dangerous criminal activity have become commonplace in the modern caviar industry. It is not uncommon for caviar shipments to be transported under armed guard, trailed by helicopters to prevent hijacking. The overfishing of sturgeon, both for its meat and roe, by illegal and legal agents, has threatened the very survival of this fish.

With the future of the sturgeon in question, there is an international effort to sustain these unique fish. A large percentage of the fish harvested from the Caspian come from artificially raised fry. Although this may seem a viable solution, the perils of life in the sea for the small baby fish, combined with the sturgeon's long maturation process, has yielded mixed results. The most promising prospects are seen in farm-raising sturgeon. Scientists at the University of California at Davis are working successfully with producers farm-raising American species of sturgeon, and similar efforts are underway in the Gironde region in France, as well as in Russia and Azerbaijan. Farm-raised sturgeon mature sooner than their wild counterparts and can be maintained in a completely clean and pollution-free environment. At this time, farm-raised caviar represents only a small part of the market, but it is the future of a sustainable supply of caviar.

CAVIAR PRODUCTION

Although all roe is processed in basically the same way to create caviar, there can be great differences in quality. The fish spawn in the spring and fall, and weather and time of year affects the catch. Most sturgeon are caught live, in nets. The fish are examined and sexed, and if judged female and full of eggs, kept alive until processing. The ideal is to harvest a fecund female when the ovaries occupy almost the whole cavity of the fish, and if a fish is not ready it may be returned to the water. Depending on the size of the fish and the resources of the fisherman, the fish are either kept in tanks on board ship or sent to be processed immediately. A key to preserving the quality of the eggs is to remove the roe sacs from a stunned fish as quickly as possible. If the fish dies and the eggs are left intact when it goes into rigor mortis, their integrity is ruined. Unfortunately, the sturgeon must be killed in order to remove the eggs. (The rest of the sturgeon is also used.) Although research is being done to develop techniques to remove eggs without sacrificing the fish, scientists have, as of yet, not found a completely satisfactory solution.

There is a fine art to producing top-quality caviar, and the caviar masters, or *ikrjanschik,* are highly respected for their skill and experience. Each fish is different, and the master will decide how to handle the eggs for maximum result. The degree of their ripeness and how the eggs are manipulated determines the ultimate quality of the caviar. The master must determine whether the eggs are perfectly ripe, immature, or too mature, and adjust the curing techniques to bring out the best in the roe.

The eggs are carefully removed from the fish. They are assigned a lot number that stays with those eggs, on their tin and their pedigree papers, all the way to their final destination. The egg sacs are gently pressed, by hand, through a fine-meshed screen to separate the delicate eggs from the membrane that holds them together. The eggs are then washed in cool water, weighed, and graded for color, size, firmness, uniformity, shine, and integrity. Grading is done exclusively by sight, based on the experience of the master, who decides the future of the eggs within minutes.

How the eggs are preserved determines their economic worth, taste, and destination. All caviar is salted, for without salt the eggs would be bland and highly perishable. The marriage of eggs and salt is what makes caviar caviar. The salt is sometimes mixed with borax, which is said to produce a caviar with a more rounded, sweeter flavor. (In the sixteenth century, caviar was placed in bags and buried in the soil near the Caspian, which is naturally rich in borax). Borax as an additive was illegal in the United States until recently. This is why many caviar connoisseurs preferred caviar in Europe, since caviar imported there is borax treated and has less salt.

There are huge differences in amounts of salt added to caviar. *Malossol,* Russian for "lightly salted," is the desired treatment for the best eggs, yielding the finest-tasting caviar, which garners the highest price in international markets. Malossol caviar can have no more than 2.8 to 3 percent salt in relation to the egg weight. Lesser-grade barrel caviar has higher percentages of salt, up to 10 percent. Traditionally, this caviar was destined for the Russian domestic market, since it was less expensive. The eggs are salted for just two to four minutes and then placed on screens to drain. Eggs can also be pasteurized after curing and packing, although heat permanently alters the eggs' delicate protein. The resulting caviar doesn't have the distinctive "pop in the mouth" connoisseurs appreciate in malassol, being more pelletlike. Pasteurized caviar is more shelf-stable and less expensive than malassol. It must be made from quality eggs, or the eggs will completely break down in processing. Eggs unsuitable for granular caviar, are used for pressed caviar, *payusuaya ikra.* This can be made from a blend of eggs and has a pronounced salty sweetness and an intense jammy texture. It is made into a sliceable cake that can also be frozen.

Caviar is packed into 1.8-kilogram drumlike tins, known in the industry as "original tins." A full original tin of caviar is impressive. The same simple design has been used for them for generations. The varnished tins are the ideal size to keep the eggs from being crushed by their own weight during long storage. The interiors are concave, which helps to expel excess brine and air. The tins are filled to about one-half inch above the rim with caviar and leveled off, then a lid is pressed on. After the caviar settles, the tins are secured by a wide, sturdy rubber band snapped around the brim of the tin, to make an airtight seal. This rubber band allows for the expansion and contraction of the tin during shipment and storage without damaging the eggs. Traditional tin colors denote the caviar species: beluga is packed in blue tins, osetra in yellow tins, and sevruga in red.

Temperature is paramount in caviar handling. Caviar should be stored between 32° and 35°F. Since fresh caviar can be stored for up to one year in its original tin, the maintenance of a cool temperature at all times is the key to successful preservation. Freezing caviar alters the texture of the egg and is a controversial practice in the caviar industry. Caviar is best consumed straight from the original tin. Repackaging into smaller containers should be done just before consuming. If you are purchasing caviar in small tins or jars, consume it within one week. Once a container is opened, you should consume the caviar within forty-eight hours. During that time, store any unused caviar with plastic wrap lightly pressed on the surface of the eggs to reduce the exposure to air.

CHOOSING AND PURCHASING CAVIAR

The taste of great caviar is unforgettable. When served chilled, the tiny beadlike capsules of premium caviar reveal a range of complex flavors and textures. Each batch of fine caviar is individual, due to the uniqueness of each sturgeon, the time of year of the catch, and the waters that give the caviar its distinctive flavor. Unfortunately, people will often swallow poor-quality caviar, either because they are inexperienced and intimidated by the cachet of caviar or don't want to ruin the moment. But anyone can recognize salty, fishy, goopy eggs. Good caviar is expensive, and any dealer worth his or her salt knows when they have a good product and will charge accordingly. Unfortunately, we can anticipate a steady rise in caviar prices due to a dwindling supply.

Buying caviar is an event that should be enjoyed. Buy from a source that turns over their stock regularly, and if possible, that repacks the caviar themselves to assure quality. Don't buy caviar that has been in a warm display case for any period of time. Strike up a conversation with the person who is selling it, ask where it comes from, and relish participating in something very special. Being cavalier about caviar does dishonor to this noble fish. It pays to inspect the caviar container for seepage and to make sure the vacuum seal is intact. If the caviar is in glass, you can see the shape and viscosity of the eggs, which should be reasonably moist and able to rotate in the jar. Ask if it's possible to have the tin opened for a visual test. The caviar should have no strong aromas, and the eggs should be of uniform size and color, without damaged membranes and with a light glossy sheen from the natural oils. Color varies tremendously and is not always a sign of full, exciting flavor. For example, albino caviar, which is a brilliant yellow, is highly prized as a rarity but has a very delicate taste. Some dealers classify their caviar by color and size, particularly beluga and osetra, but taste is the key. If possible, ask for a small taste, and insist on it if you are buying a prodigious amount of caviar. The caviar should not taste fishy, acidic, or tart, or be slimy, and if it has a murky flavor it may have been frozen. Most dealers stand behind their product, but caviar is volatile and there can be marked differences even in the best of houses.

CAVIAR GLOSSARY

Sturgeon Caviars

Beluga (*Huso huso*): The largest bead of caviar. Its flavor is mild, buttery, and rich. The rarest of all the caviars and therefore the most expensive. It can be graded 000 for the largest eggs and 00 for medium-grain eggs. The color ranges from dark black to pearly gray. This caviar, when pressed against the roof of your mouth with your tongue, should pop lightly.

Kaluga (*Huso dauricus*): The eggs of the Chinese sturgeon. They are slightly smaller than beluga and a darker black. The taste and price are comparable to beluga, but with a slightly nutty flavor. Sometimes marketed as Chinese Imperial or Beluga Prime.

Osetra (*Acipenser gueldenstaedti*): Potentially the most interesting of all the caviars. Its taste varies greatly, with complex fruity and nutty flavors that develop in the mouth with a wonderful payoff. There are different types within the species; golden, for example, which is a light yellowy gray, and reputedly from more mature fish, is known for its superlative hazelnut taste. Sea of Azov osetra can have a smokiness to it, while the newly imported black-nose karaburum (*A. gueldenstaedti persicus*) from Iran is intensely nutty. Osetra varies in color from dark gray to black to an almost golden green.

Sevruga (*Acipenser stellatus*): This caviar has less of a pop in the mouth and is more of a mass, because of its smaller and softer eggs. The flavor is sometimes described as meaty, and it has a slight citrus note. This is the most accessibly priced of all the Caspian caviars. Because of its bright flavor and salinity, it holds up to other foods more successfully than other caviars.

White sturgeon (*Acipenser transmontanus*): This caviar, from a fish farm-raised in California, is comparable in size to the Caspian osetra. Its flavor is delicate, and as a farm-raised, sustainable source it has great potential.

Paddlefish (*Polyodontidae*): From a Mississippi River–basin fish, this American sturgeon caviar, sometimes called spoonbill, is an affordable alternative to Caspian caviars. Though definitely not as complex as its Russian cousins, good-quality paddlefish caviar is refreshingly tasty.

Hackleback sturgeon (*Scaphirhynchus platorhynchus*): A medium-sized roe with a slight nuttiness, this caviar is from a smaller fish—about three feet long—that is native to the Mississippi/Missouri River basin.

OTHER FISH ROES

Salmon: Although not legally a caviar (that distinction is reserved solely for sturgeon eggs), this is the fish roe familiar to most people. Salmon roe is a wonderfully exciting food. Brightly flavored, textured eggs fully pop in the mouth and add panache to even the simplest of dishes. Its relatively low price, compared to sturgeon caviar, makes this a roe that you can enjoy abundantly.

Lumpfish: This Scandinavian roe, the queen of the supermarket caviar selections, is usually dyed with vegetable or cuttlefish ink and pasteurized. Lumpfish is to fine caviar what an interstate motel is to the Paris Ritz: They are both hotels, but the comparison dwindles after that. But sometimes I love a good low-rent overnight stay. That's the way I feel about lumpfish. Give it a little rinse and enjoy it for what it is.

Whitefish: This inexpensive roe from the Great Lakes and Canada, can vary from relatively bland to lightly sweet, with a pleasant textured crunch. Its golden color makes it a winning combination when served with other roes.

Flying fish, or tobiko: This is the darling of the sushi bar, and is used in Japanese cooking for its texture and bright color. This Caribbean fish roe, known in Japanese as *tobiko,* comes in a rainbow of dyed colors: orange, green, and red. They can also be pungently flavored with soy, ginger, or wasabi, which combines a serious horseradish kick to its crisp texture. This roe is best used in dishes that take advantage of its unique crunchy texture.

Cod: The pink roe of cod, the popular tarama of Greek cooking, is considered a delicacy by some. Salted and sold intact as a granular roe, it is available both fresh and jarred. Good-quality tarama, or cod roe, should be delicate, whereas lesser ones are acrid, with an off-putting chemical taste.

TRUFFLES

My love affair with truffles began over fifteen years ago, when I was a cook at the Quilted Giraffe. On my first night in the kitchen, I was presented with an intimidating lump of inky black dough: Ten pounds of pasta transformed by hundreds of dollars of Périgord black truffles. As I reverently passed the ebony dough through the rollers of the pasta machine, the aroma was intoxicating, the essence of pure nature, wild, funky, and implacable. Up to that point my experience with truffles was an unfulfilled promise from poorly tinned "truffled" products. This was completely different, and I was hooked.

TRUFFLE ORIGINS

These tuberlike fungi make their home in the root system of certain broad-leafed trees, primarily hazelnuts, holm oaks, lindens, willows, and poplars. The choicest truffles and the bulk of all come from France, Italy, and Spain. Lesser ones are found in Yugoslavia, China, Turkey, Northern Africa, and even America. Although there are over seventy varieties of edible truffles, the principal ones to captivate gourmands are the white truffle (*Tuber magnatum pico*) and the black winter truffle (*Tuber melanosporum*), and to a lesser extent, the summer truffle (*Tuber aestivum*).

The taste and aroma of white truffles is a heady mix of earthy sensuality mingled with pepper and garlic. More buff colored than white, and of varied round shapes, they can be as small as a thumbnail or as large as a softball, and they are the most expensive of all truffles, since they cannot be cultivated and are very rare. A top-quality freshly dug white truffle will perfume an entire room, can be smelled on the street through a closed window, and is an extraordinary dining experience. As a truffle hunter in the market in Alba told me, "The white truffle is like a dream."

Although closely associated with the Piedmont region of Italy, and sometime known as Alba or Piedmont truffles, white truffles are found throughout central Italy, including Umbria, Tuscany, the Marches, Emilia-Romagna, Lazio, Abruzzo, and Molise, and to a lesser extent in Yugoslavia.

In the fall, the air of Alba is rich with the aroma of truffles, chocolate, and roasting hazelnuts. The city fills up with truffle-loving visitors from all over the world who come for the markets and expositions and to eat truffles. The fall truffle market here is organized so that the general public can purchase truffles directly from the hunters, and unlike most truffle markets, the wares are openly displayed. (A typical truffle market is much more clandestine, with truffles and money passing back and forth like contraband.) Like most food markets, it is a social place where locals meet not just to buy and sell but to catch up with friends and gossip about truffles, dogs, and the weather, all in a cloud of truffle fragrance. A truffle *is* its aroma, and as you walk from table to table, sellers hold the truffles out under your nose, not just to induce you to buy but to share the magic of their perfume. Freshly dug truffles, close to the soil of their origin, are intoxicating.

True black winter truffles (*Tuber melanosporum*), sometimes known as Périgord truffles even if they come from other regions, taste of the woods, with a deep wine-cellar note and a hint of anise. They look like a rounded lump of coal and have a skin that's textured like a dog's nose. Black winter truffles can be indirectly cultivated with relative success, but the majority are from wild sources. They are found in abundance in the Périgord, Quercy, and Angoumois regions of France, and to a lesser extent, in the Gard, Drôme, Isère, Vaucluse, Pyrenees, Jura, Ardèche, Tricastin, and Hérault regions. In Italy, Umbria is the central homeland of black truffles, along with the Marches, Abruzzo, Molise, and Lazio.

There is a fierce rivalry concerning Italian, French, and Spanish black truffles, although the species are exactly the same and grow in very similar soils. It is not surprising that a food that tastes of the earth would generate such chauvinism and culinary patriotism. Truffle lovers also fiercely debate the superiority of black versus white truffles, a conflict that, not surprisingly, divides into French and Italian camps. The comparison is unfair; when fresh, each has its own distinctive aroma, and they are not interchangeable in the kitchen. White truffles should be enjoyed raw, while black truffles need to be warmed to fully appreciate their charms. Enjoy both for the fantastic foods that they are.

The summer truffle, sometimes called the cook's truffle or English truffle, for it was once common in England, is not as aromatic as either the white or black winter variety. It is similar in appearance to the black winter truffle, but is browner. It has a more mushroomy taste and should be drastically less expensive. The workhorse of the truffle industry, summer truffles are much more easily cultivated than their black and white cousins and are the base for most truffle products, like butters, pastas, and preserved truffles.

HOW TRUFFLES GROW

Contributing to the truffle's mystery is its precarious subterranean existence. This rootless fungus cannot be seen above ground. Before scientists were able to identify how the truffle grew, its curious appearance fostered a sinister reputation: It was thought that truffles were the devil's handiwork. The truffle fungus spreads its microscopic mycelium, or filamentlike spores, into the root system of a host tree. It is not an easy partnership, however, for to prosper a truffle needs a well-aerated alkaline-rich soil that is neither too wet nor dry, along with balmy temperatures. The truffle and the tree develop a symbiotic relationship, known as a mycorrhiza. The truffle draws nourishment from the soil to the tree, and in return the tree provides organic matter, mainly sugars. The tree doesn't benefit equally in this alliance and generally becomes dwarfed. If all goes well, the beginnings of a truffle, which looks like a tiny amber marble, will form six to eight months before it is fully mature. Typically, but not always, this creates a *brûle*, or the appearance of scorched earth, at the base of the tree where the truffle hoards the soil's nutrients. These barren circles fostered a medieval belief that the "black diamond of the kitchen" was the devil's work, grown from the spittle of witches. The *brûle* grows from year to year, and in general, the truffles are found at the outer edges of the circle.

Certain species of truffles can be cultivated indirectly. This is thanks to the experimentation of Joseph Talon, a French peasant who is considered the grandfather of truffle cultivation. In 1811, observing that truffles were always found around certain trees, Talon secretly planted their acorns on his meager plot of land. Years later, he was rewarded with a crop of truffles. Although Talon tried to keep his methods secret, word leaked out and truffle farming began in earnest in France. In Southwestern France, after vineyards where destroyed by phylloxera in the nineteenth century, truffle trees were planted in the abandoned vineyards with great success.

Modern truffle cultivation begins with planting seedlings, primarily nut and oak trees, their roots inoculated with truffle spores. The grower then waits six to ten years to see if there is a fruitful symbiosis. Truffle plantations, or *truffières,* are carefully monitored, irrigated, and guarded against poachers. The planting of a *truffière* can turn generally unproductive land into a lucrative plot. A thriving tree can produce truffles for up to thirty years, and wild trees have been known to produce for up to eighty years. But truffle farming it is not without large financial risk, and there are no guarantees.

Late-summer rains are essential for a good white and black winter truffle season. A French proverb says that if it rains and thunders on St. Bartholomew's Day (August 24), it will be a good year for truffles. The heavy rainfall needed for truffles, however, is a curse for the neighboring wine crops of Italy's Piedmont and France's Périgord and Provençal regions; in years when truffles are abundant, great wine will be scarce. This dependence on weather, soil, and host tree explains why truffles are so scarce and why there can be such huge swings in truffle harvests from year to year, which causes dramatic price fluctuations.

Ripeness is defined by a truffle's perfume, not its size or shape. A truffle can reach its full growth three months before developing its full aroma. The truffle ripens from a single spot on the peridium, or skin, which then spreads over the whole mass. A truffle's size is not a reflection of its flavor or aroma, and each one is unique. The average black winter truffle is between 1 and 2 ounces, and the size of a golf ball. White truffles range from quarter-ounce babies to a once-a-season colossus of 2 pounds. Each truffle variety has its own season, and it is important to buy and eat them at their peak of flavor. Overzealous chefs, trying to be the first to serve that year's truffles, are foolishly paying top dollar when they serve white truffles in August. True aficionados know that it is best not to push the season. If a scrupulous hunter unearths an immature truffle, he will leave it undisturbed to allow it to ripen. White truffles begin to ripen in late September or early October, are best in November, and are available until early January. Black winter truffles ripen between the first and the last frost, from November through March, peaking in January and February. Summer truffles are available from May through November.

HUNTING TRUFFLES

Since truffles cannot be seen, they are not harvested but hunted. The hunters—the colorful *trifolau* of Italy and the *rabassiers* of southern France—track the ripe truffle's profound perfume through the woods. Unfortunately, humans don't have the sensitivity needed to perceive the truffle's aroma through a foot or more of dirt. To pinpoint a truffle, hunters have relied over the years on the keen noses of pigs and dogs. Pigs are natural truffle hunters, particularly sows, which are attracted by the tuber's pheromonelike scent. (Pheromones are aromatic chemicals that transmit primal, sometimes sexual, messages between species.) Although pigs are trainable, hunters have to fight with their porcine partners for their finds. On top of that, it's a little tricky to pack a couple of hundred pounds of pig into a small Peugeot or Fiat.

Generally, truffle hunters use trained dogs when foraging. There is no specific breed for truffling; some hunters claim the low-to-the-ground dachshund is best, while others prefer German shepherds. Trained as puppies, the dogs are groomed for the specific task and discipline of finding the elusive truffle without destroying it. This is not an easy mission, and it can take years for the dogs to perfect their skills. The hunter-dog relationship is at the heart of finding truffles, and a good dog is a prized animal. One desired quality in a good truffle dog is the shape of its paws, which shouldn't be turned too far in or out. The dog must learn to dig just with the pads of its paws, making a small hole to get the truffle. If the dog breaks up the ground too much, it disturbs the subterranean structure of the truffle mycorrhizae, preventing future fruiting. Many dogs learn to hold the delicate truffle in their mouths without breaking or biting it. It can take hours of searching before truffles are found, and the dog must stay focused. Some hunters prefer white dogs in order to see them in the dark of night, when most truffle hunting happens. In the truffle regions of both France and Italy, truffle-dog shows and competitions to identify the quickest truffle hound are a big part of truffle season. There are experienced hunters, however, who can unearth truffles without the aid of either pigs or dogs. Instead they scour known truffle grounds on their hands and knees, in search of the truffle flies that congregate just over the spot where a truffle is growing.

Another reason dogs have replaced pigs is that hunting with a dog is much more discreet. Truffle hunting is a serious cash business, and a talented hunter can make good money finding these delicacies that only days later will be served in the finest restaurants of New York, Tokyo, and Paris. A large part of the truffle economy is underground, with cash changing hands undocumented. Truffle prices fluctuate daily with the velocity of the stock market. Many hunters are older men, independent folks who make their living from the land and are adamant about keeping the government from dipping its fingers into their earnings.

Truffle hunters are not just avoiding the tax man, but each other as well. Truffle-producing spots in the woods are well-guarded secrets, and competition is fierce. In bad truffle years, there are disturbing stories of truffle dogs being poisoned to take a hunter out of the game. The legend is that the best hunter is the oldest son of a recently deceased truffle hunter, for only on his death bed would a seasoned hunter reveal the location of his most fruitful spots. Serious hunting goes on at night to keep the location of the best truffle-producing trees secret.

TRUFFLE VARIETIES

Black winter truffle (*Tuber melanosporum*), also called Périgord, Umbrian, or Rabasse truffle: From southwest and southern France, Italy (Umbria, Piedmont, the Marches, Abruzzo, Molise, and Lazio), and the Lalbenque region of Spain. Can be as small as a walnut or as big as a man's fist, but the average size is 1 to 2 ounces, golf ball size. Blackish-chocolate or chestnut-black, with a uniformly textured skin like a dog's nose. If it has a reddish cast, it is not ripe and not worth the money. It should be firm and not spongy, without mold. The interior (gleba), when ripe, should be purplish black, marked with a fine white-lined marbled pattern. Available fresh November to March; the best part of the season is January 15 through February 15. Available year-round frozen, or preserved in pastes, butter, pasta, and juice.

Summer truffle (*Tuber aestivum*), also called English truffle, or cook's truffle: Found in Spain, France, Italy, and Southern Germany. Reminiscent of its winter cousin, it is blackish, with a brown or sometimes yellowish-brown veiny interior. This truffle has a milder aroma with more of a mushroomy flavor, and lacks the pungency and sexiness of the melanosporum. Though it is much less expensive, it also is a real disappointment if you are thinking true melanosporum, but it is pleasant fresh in the summer. When preserved, its flavor ranges from muted to musky to nonexistent. Available fresh May through November, or frozen. Used extensively in truffled products.

Musk truffle (*Tuber brumale*), also called brumale or magenta truffle: Harvested at the same time as melanosporum, this truffle can be a grower's bane if its spores invade a melanosporum orchard. A deeper black, and sometimes browner, it doesn't have the melanosporum flavor and is not as dense. Its aroma is similar to aestivum, yet more musky. Some varieties are acrid and bitter. This truffle is sometimes available fresh, but it is usually found canned, preserved, or used to flavor cheeses.

Burgundy truffle (*Tuber uncinatum*): Common in Burgundy and Lorraine. Closely related to aestivum, with a delicate, pleasant perfume. Harvested in the fall. When perfectly ripe, the flesh is chocolate-cherry colored, with a more open internal vein pattern than the melanosporum.

White truffle (*Tuber magnatum pico*), also called Alba, Piemonte, or Aqualange truffle: Found in Italy, in the Piedmont, Umbria, Tuscany, the Marches, Emilia-Romagna, Lazio, Abruzzo, and Molise—and to a lesser extent in Yugoslavia. A creamy beige color, occasionally with a reddish tinge. Red indicates a willow-tree host, believed by cognoscenti to yield a finer truffle. The most expensive truffle and, when you have a fresh specimen, the headiest of them all. It tastes like sex. It impregnates the air with an unforgettable aroma. It resists cultivation. Best consumed fresh, as the aroma fades dramatically within a couple of days. These truffles are preserved, but not without compromising their flavor. They should be consumed within 5 to 7 days of harvest.

Tuscan truffle (*Tuber albidium pico or Tuber borchii*), also called "bianchetti": A whitish truffle found in Emilia-Romagna, Lazio, and from Tuscany down to Campagna. Found in the spring, and early summer. Light brown to dirty white in color, it is known as the poor man's white truffle. Often used in canned white-truffle products, so check labels carefully. Can be great or taste unpleasantly chemical.

Oregon white truffles (*Tuber gibbosum*): Native Oregonian James Beard was a big fan of this truffle. The aroma can be cheesy, or smell of freshly roasted hazelnuts and spices. Best in October and November. Sold fresh and preserved.

Oregon black truffle (*Leucangium carthusiana*): Not a true truffle, but appreciated by Pacific Northwest loyalists for its rich, mushroomy chocolate taste. Available fresh.

Chinese truffles (*Tuber indicum, Tuber sinese, and Tuber himilayense*), also called Himalayan truffles: These truffles grow in the Szechwan province of China as well as in Pakistan. Indicum looks like a chocolate truffle, but lacks any distinguishing taste. Sinese has a chewy texture and an oily, almost gassy aroma with a bitter aftertaste. Harvested at the same time as melanosporum, they are much less expensive. There are stories that unscrupulous sellers pad their supplies of melanosporum with these truffles, since they can pick up the perfume of the true winter black truffle. Unfortunately, they don't have the same flavor. If packed covered with their native dirt, the dirt will be reddish, indicating a warning to the savvy consumer.

BUYING TRUFFLES AND TRUFFLE PRODUCTS

If you can't hunt for truffles, buying a fresh truffle is the next best thing. When purchasing fresh truffles, first check with your source to find out when the truffles were delivered. (Typically, truffles are delivered at the end of the week for weekend indulgences.) If they have been in the store for a week, they aren't worth their high price. Truffles begin to lose their pungency within a couple days of being dug, so you want to use them as soon as possible.

Don't buy a truffle without smelling and inspecting it, and if you are buying a number of them, check every one. A truffle should be fully perfumed; if you have to hunt for its aroma, it is over the hill. It should be firm and not spongy. It may be covered with dirt, so rub the dirt off to make sure you have a good and true specimen. (Truffle hunters can be tricky, sticking two small truffles or some broken bits together with twigs and covering them with mud.)

When you purchase a truffle, take it home, wrap it loosely in a paper towel, and store it in an airtight jar. Change the paper daily. Try placing a couple of eggs or some butter in the jar with the truffle to perfume them. Use the truffle as soon as you can. A white truffle can last up to a week and black truffles up to 2 weeks, but their aroma weakens every day.

If you can't find or afford fresh truffles, there are other ways to enjoy their taste. Flash-freezing black winter truffles is the best way to preserve these truffles. They are not as pungent as the fresh, but deliver a good truffle taste. Slice them while frozen and add to sauces. Whether frozen, canned, or jarred, preserved white truffles are a disappointment.

Black winter truffles are canned and jarred sliced, in bits, or whole, with various degrees of success. Anyone who knows truffles will tell you that the simple act of preserving them, which heats the truffle, dissipates its aroma and taste. Preserved truffles should be used as an accent, not the central player in a dish. Many preserved truffle products have a high proportion of less-expensive summer truffles, which don't deliver a lot of flavor. Check the label to make sure what truffles are being used in the product. A good and reasonably priced product is black truffle juice. Although not actually the juice of a truffle, but the water used in preserving the truffle, it adds a welcome earthiness to sauces. Dried truffle powder tastes like dirt without any of the sophistication of truffles and is not worth its price.

Most Americans experience truffles in flavored butters and oils. These have a pungency that, when used judiciously, can add a truffly background flavor. Unfortunately, the truffle mania that has swept American kitchens has led chefs to use these products indiscriminately. Butters and oils are affordable and are a great introduction to truffles, but once you have had fresh truffles these products pale by comparison. The stark reality, according to Olga Urbani of the famous Umbrian family that for four generations has been the world leader in fresh and quality preserved truffle products, is that you can't use real truffles in commercial truffle oils. Fresh truffles stored in oil for long periods of time go rancid. Commercially produced truffle oils rely on simulated truffle flavors instead. The components of those flavors are patented trade secrets. Truffle butters are made mostly with summer truffles, but they also can vary in quality and a little goes a long way in a dish.

Truffle cheeses from Périgord, Piedmont, and Umbria are becoming very popular, as anything truffled has extra cachet. Some of these are interesting, but many use a whiff of truffle to boost an ordinary cheese. Sheep and cow's milk tend to work best with the aroma of truffles. When buying these cheeses, make sure that they have a full truffle aroma. Sottocenere al tartufo, a semi-soft cow's-milk cheese flavored with truffles and spices and Tartufello, from Siena, with a robust truffle taste, are both recommended.

Handling truffles is easy. Leave any dirt on the truffle until ready to use it. Clean it under tepid running water with a brush. (I use a soft toothbrush to get into the textured surface.) Some chefs peel the nubbly skin of the truffle, but I like to leave its natural shape intact since the skin is thoroughly edible. It is best to slice a truffle tissue-paper-thin or mince it to create as much surface area as possible. There are special truffle slicers shaped like small paddles with a sharp blade that you run the truffle over, which make slicing wonderfully easy. You can also use a mandoline or a sharp chef's knife. The truffle should not be sliced or cut until right before you use it. If you have any leftover white truffle, mix it with a little oil and use it within a day. If you are fortunate enough to have an excess of leftover black truffle, mix it with enough unsalted butter so that it looks like chocolate-chip ice cream and freeze it, well wrapped, until ready to use, or mix it with oil and use it within a day or so. Whole black truffles can also be well wrapped and frozen, but much of their texture and perfume will be lost.

When you have truffles, don't hoard them, enjoy them, relish them. A truffle isn't just an expensive trophy, but an opportunity to really taste and connect with something wild and unadulterated. A true rarity.

FOIE GRAS

A taste of foie gras is an unforgettable experience. Foie gras, with its French appellation, is a calling card of luxury. Foie gras—"fat liver" in English—is the enlarged liver of a fattened duck or goose. This mundane definition belies the extravagant nature of this food, for to imagine it as the same as liver with onions is like calling the great diva Maria Callas just a singer. No other food offers its silken, sinful richness, and sublime taste. People who normally turn up their noses at liver savor foie gras. Preparations of this food represent the epitome of the French haute cuisine and in America have come to be a signature of serious restaurant kitchens.

Foie gras (pronounced *fwah grah*) is produced by force-feeding (*gavage* in French) geese or ducks with grain. The birds are put on a progressive force-feeding regimen for the final two to four weeks before they are butchered, which causes the liver to expand from a couple of ounces to around 1 pound for ducks and as much as 2 pounds for geese. This process also completely changes the nature of the liver. A standard liver, with its maroon hue and potentially bitter flavor, is transformed into a buff-colored, buttery, nutty meat without a trace of harshness.

THE HISTORY OF FOIE GRAS

The roots of foie gras production go back to the Nile Delta in ancient Egypt, where the goose was revered as a symbol of the connection between man and the divine. Domesticated geese were a mainstay of the ancient barnyard as waddling reservoirs of fat, tasty meat and comforting down. Like the pig, almost every part of the goose could be used. It is believed that hunters discovered that migrating geese naturally gorged themselves before their long

northern flight, resulting in both excess body fat as well as a transformed liver. Farmers working on this cue from nature developed accelerated feeding methods to fatten their birds, not for the livers but for the valuable cooking fat. Tomb relief paintings from around 2300 B.C. depict farmers force-feeding geese pellets of grain. Historically, high-calorie fats were a scarcity that humans sought out to supplement a lean vegetable-based diet. It may be hard for modern Americans to imagine a shortage of fat in the diet, but this was the case for most of human history. Fat was a luxury, not a fast-food convenience.

The force-feeding of domesticated geese and ducks was practiced in both Greece and Rome. Romans improved on the Egyptian methods, feeding geese specifically for their livers. They developed a system that used dried figs instead of grain, which produced a sweeter, more delicate liver, close in taste and texture to the foie gras of today. This method became so prevalent that the Latin phrase for an enlarged goose liver, *iecur ficatum*, took its root from *ficus* (fig), which is also the root of modern Romance-language words for liver: the French *foie*, the Spanish *higado*, and the Italian *fegato*. Foie gras became a Roman symbol of luxury and of human mastery of the natural world.

With the fall of the Roman Empire, luxurious feasts and high living essentially took a millennium-long hiatus. The techniques for making foie gras were not lost, however, though there are different views on how they were passed on. One theory is that foie gras techniques continued to be practiced on a very small scale by the peasantry of Gascony, in southwestern France, following their Roman occupation. Another compelling school of thought, wonderfully outlined by Michael Ginor and Mitchell Davis in their detailed *Foie Gras: A Passion* (John Wiley and Sons, 1999) is that the techniques were maintained as part of the culinary traditions of Ashkenazi Jews in Central and Western Europe.

Enslaved Jews in Roman-occupied Palestine would have learned the techniques for force-feeding geese from the Romans. This skill became an important asset. Jewish dietary law imposes strict restrictions on the types of fat allowed in cooking. Beef and pork lard are not kosher, and butter cannot be mixed with meat. Poultry fat, however, is acceptable. In their traditional homeland, Mediterranean Jews could rely on a rich supply of olive and seed oils to use in cooking. In the diaspora, however, Jews who migrated to Northern Europe had to rely on alternative sources for cooking oil. Rendered chicken fat, or *schmaltz,* became an ideal economical choice. Besides chickens, geese were traditional livestock on German and Hungarian farms, and when force-fed for only a few weeks, provided a fantastic source of fat for Jewish communities.

On the eve of the Renaissance, foodways took on a whole new drama and importance in the lives of the privileged classes of Western Europe. Interest in luxuries like foie gras and truffles renewed. Foie gras began to be produced for courtly kitchens using techniques outlined in Roman cookery and agricultural texts. Jewish farmers were reputed to produce the finest fattened livers. According to Ginor and Davis, "Foie gras was the meeting point for disparate culinary cultures, the innovative cuisine of the European elites, and the traditional cooking of Jewish farmers and townspeople."

These parallel paths of foie gras consumption continued, and a rich foie gras tradition developed at the tables of the rich and royal. In the elaborate French cuisine of the seventeenth and eighteenth centuries, foie gras entered the classic repertoire of court chefs as a garnish to innumerable dishes. Foie gras was also paired with Périgord truffles in pâtés in an ultimate expression of culinary luxury. In a world without refrigeration, pâtés and terrines had the advantage of preserving foie gras for the short term, making it more accessible to a wider bourgeois audience throughout Europe and even America. We still see the effect of this today, for a common misconception is that foie gras is synonymous with pâté.

Foie gras became a cornerstone of the French culinary repertoire, both in the traditional cuisine of southwestern France and in the Alsace region along the German border, and in elite restaurants. In southwestern France, the production of foie gras remains an important part of the regional identity, being both a commercial and a cottage industry. There are special foie gras markets from October to April for local producers both large and small. The raising of geese and ducks traditionally was a woman's responsibility. Although the feeding regimen can be standardized, there is an art to the successful production of foie gras, and local women, called *gaveuses*, develop a reputation for their skill and knowledge. The best approach this work with pride and loving respect for the animals. It is not uncommon for the women on small farms to fatten up a couple of geese for their family and friends' Christmas tables, or as a side business to supplement the family income.

MODERN PRODUCTION

Over the last thirty years, foie gras production has advanced and now employs modern techniques of animal husbandry. The disease-resistant moulard duck has replaced the more delicate goose as a primary source of foie gras. This duck is a cross between a female Pekin and a Muscovy male. The moulard (from the French word for mule) is sterile, but brings desirable qualities from each breed. Corn, either ground to a mash, dried, or in enriched pellets, is the feed of choice. France is the leader in foie gras production and consumption. Israel, Hungary, Austria, and Poland are major producers as well.

Although there was some limited production of foie gras by German-American farmers in the nineteenth century, goose as a commercial food never really caught on in the United States. Our big bird was the turkey. By the twentieth century, Americans' exposure to foie gras was limited to tinned terrines stateside, or on holidays at the finest restaurants on the Continent. Fresh foie gras was unavailable to American chefs due to strict restrictions on the importation of fresh poultry products. That changed in the early 1980s, when a dynamic Israeli, Izzy Yaney, began producing duck foie gras on a farm a couple of hours north of New York City.

Yaney's vision was to bring foie gras to the American market, and his goal jibed with the revolution in American food. It was a time when young Americans were beginning to create an exciting new cuisine, inspired by the passion and the fine food traditions of France and Italy but with a decidedly American personality. I was working in a New American restaurant, Hubert's, in the early eighties. I remember the day a thoroughly likable young man, George Faison, brought us one of Yaney's fresh foies gras. Faison, who was just starting a business distributing quality game, meats, and pâté, was like a kid who had scored the best treat at a candy store when he showed us that foie gras. The excitement in the kitchen was palpable, for as cooks we were beginning to see the kind of quality ingredients that had for so long been out of reach. Today, Faison, along with co-owner Ariane Daguin, daughter of one of France's premier foie gras chefs, runs D'Artagnan, the definitive distributor of foie gras and game in the United States.

Those first years were not without challenges for Yaney. He persevered through a dissolved relationship with an original partner, and production setbacks—like the time in 1992 when the roof of the coop fell in ten days before Thanksgiving, killing 70 percent of their duck stock. Today, Yaney and partner Michael Ginor's Hudson Valley Foie Gras is the primary source of foie gras in America. The accessibility of quality domestic foie gras has transformed fine dining in this country. In 1999, importation restrictions were lifted on foie gras, and now cooks can choose from our own homegrown foie gras and French and Canadian products.

Foie gras does not come without controversy. It is attacked by both healthful nutrition advocates and champions of animal rights. Foie gras admittedly is rich in fat, and an analysis of a diet based simply on calories would suggest that consumption of it be limited. The reality, of course, is that most people eat foie gras only on special occasions. No one would suggest a dietary change from a weekly dish of pasta to foie gras every Wednesday night. Also to be considered is the kind of fat in foie gras. To simplify the issue, there are "good" and "bad" fats that interact with the body's blood-serum level of cholesterol. High blood-serum levels of cholesterol are linked with heart disease. Foie gras is two-thirds monounsaturated fat, the good kind of fat, which is consistent with a healthful diet. The remaining saturated fats are tempered by the presence of oleic acid, a component of monounsaturated fat.

The argument that the process of force feeding is abusive is a complicated issue and one that requires individual decision. Individual food choices reflect our beliefs, and everyone must make choices that they are comfortable with. It is important to respect and honor all the creatures that nourish us, and we shouldn't eat anything without considering the effect it has on ourselves and the environment.

Foie gras producers unequivocally state that the process of force-feeding is not unduly cruel to the animal. In fact, the *gaveuses* of France talk lovingly of the birds in their charge. Geese and ducks are very sensitive to any change or stress in environment, and great care is taken to maintain a favorable habitat for these birds. (Not only for human reasons but for economic ones, for if the ducks are stressed they do not produce top-quality livers, which command the best prices.) Studies show that ducks and geese recognize faces, and that they react more strongly to the veterinarian or a stranger than to their feeder. In the feeding, a funnel with a small electric motor is placed in the duck's esophagus and a small portion of grain, about one ounce, is poured into the tube. The duck's esophagus is made of a hard surface like a fingernail, and the placement of the tube is not painful. The electric motor moves the food into the crop of the bird and the feeder then removes the tube. The process lasts about 30 seconds, and is repeated two or three times a day. When I observed this process, it was done very calmly, without malice, and the birds did not seem to be under any duress.

BUYING FOIE GRAS

Fresh whole foies gras are available at specialty groceries around the winter holidays and by special order at other times of the year, as well as through Internet and mail-order sources. Generally, all fresh foie gras in the United States is duck. Imported French goose foie gras is available, but even by foie gras standards it is very expensive. There are two different styles of foie gras production, one that force-feeds the ducks for two weeks and another for four. Both methods produce wonderful livers but with different qualities. Livers from the shorter feeding process tend to be less veiny and are better suited for lower-heat cooking methods, such as baking in terrines, torchons, or oven roasting. These livers are produced in Canada and in France, and are sold under the labels Le Bec Fin and Quercy. The longer feeding regime produces livers, typical of Hudson Valley foie gras, with a more pronounced vein structure. These livers can be used in any preparation, but are ideal for quick high heat methods like sautéing and grilling. The veins need to be carefully removed from either style of liver before being cooked in terrines or roasted whole. Ask your butcher which style of foie gras he has available.

Impeccably fresh foie gras can be stored for up to 10 days in the refrigerator. Fresh foie gras should never be frozen, for the deep chill destroys its cell structure, causing it to liquefy when cooked. Keep foie gras in its original vacuum packaging, or well wrapped in plastic wrap, because it can discolor when exposed to the air.

There are three different grades of fresh foie gras of either style. Grade-A duck foie gras, which is the top-quality liver, is white, firm, and must weigh over 1 pound. The liver should have no blemishes, be round, and when pressed should give slightly but not be spongy. This is the liver of choice for many chefs and can be used in any preparation, including sautéing, grilling, or poaching. Grade-A livers should always be selected when making terrines or using any other low-heat method of cooking, because they render less fat.

A grade-B duck foie gras weighs less than 1 pound and tends to be softer and flatter. It renders more fat, making it undesirable for terrines and torchons. Grade-B livers are ideal for quick sautés and other high-heat methods of cooking. Some grade-B livers can be as good as a larger grade-A, however, and are appraised lower only because of their smaller size. Savvy buyers can save money by purchasing top-quality grade-B livers.

Grade-C duck foie gras is generally not available to the retail market, although it can be special ordered. This liver is suited for emulsions, mousses, and pâtés.

When you buy fresh foie gras, generally you have to buy it whole. Some purveyors, however, will sell half a liver, or a single lobe. Around the holidays you can also buy foie gras presliced in medallions ready for sautéing.

Prepared Foie Gras: Buying a slab of foie gras to spread on toast or to finish off a salad is a wonderful way to experience the lusciousness of the food without any cooking.

　　　　Foie Gras d'Oie Entier, or *Foie Gras de Canard Entier:* This is the whole liver of a goose or duck cooked and preserved. It is 100 percent foie gras, without fillers. Considered the best of the imported prepared products.

- *Bloc Foie Gras de Canard,* or *Foie Gras d'Oie:* Made from pieces formed together with whipped foie gras.

- *Mousse* or *Parfait de Foie Gras:* This is foie gras ground or pureed in order to make a smooth, creamy mousse. Available from both European and American producers.

- *Pâté de Foie Gras:* Made with other meats, like pork, duck, and veal. Generally it contains a larger portion of other meats, with a small amount of the foie gras. Be careful reading labels; if they say *duck liver* or *goose liver,* in English, these pâtés are not made with foies gras, but regular poultry livers.

HANDLING FOIE GRAS

Preparing foie gras is really quite easy as long as you are careful with temperatures. If you work with it cold, straight from the refrigerator, it is hard and difficult to cut. Let it warm slightly first: 10 minutes for slicing medallions and up to 1 hour to devein it for a terrine. Always take into consideration the heat of the day, for like butter, if foie gras becomes too warm it will begin to liquefy. If you feel the foie gras becoming flabby or a bit slippery, return it to the refrigerator.

When you remove the foie from its vacuum packaging, rinse it and pat it dry. A whole foie gras is composed of two lobes, one larger than the other. For most recipes, you will separate the two lobes by pulling gently. Check on the underside, not the rounded side, where the two lobes connect, to make sure there are no telltale green spots of bile; if they are present remove them with the tip of a knife. There may be a small fatty piece of membrane present where the two lobes connect, as well; this should be discarded. There is no need to peel the outer membrane of the foie gras.

Cutting Foie Gras into Medallions: Lay the foie gras on a cutting board so the rounded side is facing up. Heat a sharp slicing knife in warm water. Dry the knife before each slice. Starting at the narrower end of the liver, cut at an angle to make a medallion that is ½ to ¾ inch thick and 2 to 3 inches across. If the liver is very tapered at the end, the first cut can be at quite an oblique angle. Continue to cut more medallions, adjusting the angle of the cuts as you slice through the broader sections of the liver. It is always better to err on the side of the medallions being thicker rather than thinner, for if they are too thin they will cook too quickly and render away. There is no need to remove obvious veins when sautéing or grilling.

Deveining a Whole Foie Gras: Let the foie gras sit at room temperature until soft and malleable, about 1 hour. Separate the larger lobe from the smaller one by gently pulling them apart. Place the smooth side of the foie gras on a work surface. Find the spot in the larger lobe where the veins surface. With a small paring knife, pry the foie gras open and follow the major veins into the liver. The veins form tributaries from a central main core. Remove the veins from the liver by pulling gently, using small pliers if needed. Take care not to break up the liver too much. Scrape any red blemishes from the liver. Rinse and pat dry with a towel. Reshape the liver. Repeat with the smaller lobe.

COOKING FOIE GRAS

When preparing foie gras keep in mind that it doesn't behave like other meats, which can get tough as shoe leather if overcooked. Foie gras, however, because of its high fat content softens and melts if overcooked; it literally renders away. Foie gras is rarely cooked beyond medium rare. When the livers are cooked by direct heat methods, like sautéing or grilling, it is vital to do it purposefully, at high heat. Although this may seem contrary, it assures that the liver cooks quickly. Subtleties, like preheating the pan before sautéing a medallion, do make a difference, and guarantee a burnished crust before the interior of the foie gras overcooks. Other strategies are to cook it gently at a very low temperature, as in terrines. Fast or slow, the goal is to keep foie gras from overcooking and releasing its delicious essence.

AMUSE-GUEULES

A universal gesture of hospitality is the offer of a little something to eat. These inviting tastes have many names: hors d'oeuvre, tapas, mezze, nibbles, noshes. My favorite tag is the French *amuse-gueule* (roughly translated as "to amuse the mouth"). Delight your guests and set the mood is exactly what these dishes do. When you play with caviar, foie gras, and truffles, the mood can't help but be a little luxurious, too. One of these dishes, shared with an aperitif, should catch any guest's attention, be it elegant Figs Stuffed with Foie Gras Mousse, White-Truffled Grissini, or surprising Avocado and Wasabi-Tobiko Dip with Asian Vegetables.

❧

Figs Stuffed with Foie Gras Mousse

Salmon Rillettes with Corn Pancakes

Avocado and Wasabi-Tobiko Dip with Asian Vegetables

Sweet Potato Chips with American-Caviar Dip

Beach Plum and Foie Gras Canapés

White-Truffled Grissini

Foie Gras Mousse

FIGS STUFFED WITH FOIE GRAS MOUSSE

I was once told that a successful amuse-gueule—*little treats served before a meal—is like the opening line of a novel: It should catch your attention and set a tone for things to come. When fresh figs are in season, I serve them stuffed with foie gras as the "Call me Ishmael" of a celebratory feast.*

SERVES 4 TO 6

1 pound fresh Black Mission or green figs

2 ounces prepared or homemade foie gras mousse (page 59)

2 teaspoons verjus (available in specialty foods stores), or 1 teaspoon white wine vinegar diluted with 1 teaspoon water

1 tablespoon sliced almonds, toasted and finely chopped (recipe follows)

1. Trim the stem end of the figs. With the tip of a serrated apple corer, a melon baller, or a grapefruit knife, cut a small round out of the bottom of each fig and reserve. Carefully scoop about one-third of the flesh from the center of each fig and reserve.

2. In a heavy-duty mixer fitted with the paddle attachment or with a handheld mixer, beat the foie gras mousse or prepared foie gras until it is light, like a buttercream icing. Put the mousse or foie gras in a pastry bag and pipe it into the figs. Plug each fig with a reserved round piece of fig. Refrigerate for at least 1 hour, or until the mousse or foie gras is firm.

3. In a small pan, heat the reserved fig flesh with the verjus or vinegar mixture until liquefied. Press through a fine-meshed sieve to remove the seeds.

4. To serve, cut each fig in half lengthwise and brush the cut side with the glaze. Sprinkle with the toasted almonds and serve.

TOASTING NUTS

Preheat the oven to 375°F. Spread nuts on a baking sheet. Bake until brown, about 5 to 10 minutes, depending upon size.

SALMON RILLETTES WITH CORN PANCAKES

One of my favorite dinners as a young cooking student in Paris was a crusty baguette slathered with pork rillettes. This classic charcuterie is unconscionably fatty. I still love it, but today, I make a lighter version with fresh and smoked salmon studded with salmon roe. Although you can use pristine slices of smoked salmon for this, look for less-expensive smoked salmon trimmings at your fish market or deli counter. Serve the rillettes with corn pancakes, black bread, crackers, or sliced cucumbers.

MAKES ABOUT 2 CUPS; SERVES 6 TO 8

1 lemon, thinly sliced

5 to 7 large dill sprigs, plus 2 teaspoons minced fresh dill

5 to 7 large flat-leaf parsley sprigs

2 to 3 tarragon sprigs, plus 2 teaspoons minced fresh tarragon

5 ounces center-cut salmon fillet, pin bones removed

Kosher salt and freshly ground pepper to taste

4 ounces smoked salmon, chopped

2 teaspoons Dijon mustard

1 scallion, including green parts, minced

⅔ cup crème fraîche or sour cream

2 rounded tablespoons (about 1 ounce) salmon roe

Corn Pancakes (recipe follows)

1. Place a collapsible steamer in a medium pot. Add water to the pot to reach the bottom of the steamer. Line the steamer with the lemon slices and herb sprigs. Bring the water to a boil, place the salmon on the bed of herbs, cover, and steam the fish for 5 minutes. Turn off the heat and let the fish cook for 1 minute, undisturbed. The fish should be firm but not flaky, with a moist center.

2. Remove the fish from the steamer, peel off the skin, and break the fillet apart, taking care to remove any bones. Sprinkle the fish with salt and pepper. Let cool to room temperature.

3. In a food processor, puree the salmon with the minced herbs, smoked salmon, Dijon mustard, and scallion until smooth. Add the crème fraîche or sour cream and pulse just to combine. Do not overwork the mixture once the crème fraîche or sour cream is added, or the rillettes will be curdy. Season with salt and pepper to taste.

4. Transfer the rillettes to a medium bowl. Gently fold in the salmon roe, taking care not to burst the beads. Place the rillettes in a serving crock or ramekin and refrigerate for 2 hours, or until firm.

CORN PANCAKES

Henry and Sue Smith of Sycamore Farms are two of the many special growers at the Union Square Green Market in New York City. They pick their corn at dawn in Middletown, New York, and rush it down the Thruway so we city folks can appreciate the remarkable flavor of fresh corn. Often, after a meal of their splendid corn, I have a lone ear to use up, which led to this recipe. I love to serve these instead of blini. The bits of kernels provide a little pop to the texture of the cakes. These are great with caviar or foie gras, or brushed with a little truffle butter.

MAKES ABOUT 20 SMALL PANCAKES; SERVES 4 TO 6

⅓ **cup all-purpose flour**

⅓ **cup stone-ground yellow cornmeal**

½ **teaspoon baking powder**

⅛ **teaspoon baking soda**

½ **teaspoon kosher salt**

1 **teaspoon sugar**

1 **ear fresh corn, shucked**

¾ **cup buttermilk**

2 **tablespoons plus 2 teaspoons unsalted butter, melted**

1 **large egg, separated**

(continued on next page)

1. Sift the flour, cornmeal, baking powder, baking soda, salt, and sugar into a medium bowl and whisk together.

2. Cut the corn kernels from the cob. Scrape the cobs with a knife to remove the remaining milky corn pulp. In a small food processor, puree half the corn kernels and corn pulp, and the buttermilk. Add the 2 tablespoons butter and the egg yolk and pulse to combine. Stir the wet ingredients into the dry ingredients to make a thick batter. In a medium bowl, beat the egg white until soft peaks form. Fold the egg white and kernels into the batter. To ensure light cakes, take care not to overmix the batter.

3. Heat a griddle or large, heavy skillet over medium heat and brush with 1 teaspoon of the remaining butter. Drop rounded tablespoons of the batter on the griddle or the pan to make pancakes about 2 inches in diameter. Cook until golden brown on the bottom, then turn and brown on the other side. Repeat with the remaining butter and batter. Serve warm.

AVOCADO AND WASABI-TOBIKO DIP WITH ASIAN VEGETABLES

One summer, I lived in a house in Berkeley, California, that had a prolific avocado tree in the backyard. It was a challenge keeping up with the bounty of falling avocados, which could quickly cover the patio with guacamole. In defense, I developed a repertoire of quick dips to use up the bumper crop of fruit. This is one of my favorites, because it is both unexpected and incredibly easy.

SERVES 4

DIP:

1 avocado, pitted and peeled

½ teaspoon grated peeled fresh ginger

3 tablespoons wasabi tobiko

1 tablespoon minced red onion

2 tablespoons minced fresh cilantro

1 tablespoon fresh lime juice

½ teaspoon kosher salt

DIPPERS:

1 yellow bell pepper, seeded, deribbed, and cut into strips

2 ounces snow peas, strings removed

1 Kirby (unwaxed pickling) cucumber, thinly sliced

2-inch piece daikon, peeled and thinly sliced

Thin rice crackers (not rice cakes)

1. To make the dip: Put the avocado in a medium bowl. Add the ginger, tobiko, onion, cilantro, lime juice, and salt. With a large fork, smash all the ingredients together to make a coarse-textured dip.

2. Transfer the dip to a small serving bowl. Set the bowl on a large plate and arrange the dippers on the plate. Serve immediately.

SWEET POTATO CHIPS WITH AMERICAN-CAVIAR DIP

Chips and dip are as American as I Love Lucy, Disney, *and Michael* Jordan. *They combine crisp and creamy, sweet and salty, familiar and comforting. Even my young daughter, who avoids food in most forms, will devour a bowl of these chips with the zeal of a QVC shopper. Here a dip gets gussied up with a generous helping of caviar. For a more colorful spread, use a combination of black, red, or white roe. If using a black whitefish or lumpfish roe, don't skip the step of rinsing the eggs before combining them in the dip.*

MAKES ABOUT 1 CUP; SERVES 4 TO 6

CHIPS:

4 cups vegetable oil for deep-frying

1 large sweet potato, peeled (about 1½ pounds)

Wondra flour for dredging

Fine sea salt

DIP:

¾ cup sour cream

¾ cup cream cheese, at room temperature

1 tablespoon minced scallions

¾ cup American whitefish or lumpfish roe, well rinsed and drained if roe is black

Freshly ground pepper to taste

1. Pour 2 to 3 inches of oil into a large, heavy saucepan. The oil should fill the pan no more than one-third full. This will prevent the oil from bubbling over when frying the potatoes. Heat the oil over medium-high heat to 340°F. Lay out 3 layers of paper towel on a baking sheet or large pan.

(continued on next page)

2. While the oil is heating, make the chips: Using a mandoline, slice a third of the sweet potato very thin, about ⅟₁₆ inch thick. Toss the sweet potato slices with the flour. Place a large handful of the slices in a medium-mesh sieve and shake off the excess flour. Hold the sieve over the hot oil and carefully drop the slices into the oil. Do not dip the sieve into the oil. (Do not look into the pot after dropping the slices, because there will be an initial blast of hot steam.) Stir the slices a couple times as they fry. When the oil has stopped bubbling and the slices are light brown and crisp, use a skimmer to transfer them to paper towels to drain. Repeat with the remaining slices. Season with sea salt to taste. (The chips can be made 1 day ahead and stored at room temperature in an airtight container.)

3. To make the dip: In a medium bowl, whisk the sour cream and cream cheese together until completely smooth. Fold in the scallions and roe. Season with pepper. Serve with the chips. (To make ahead, refrigerate for up to 1 hour.)

There are no bargains in caviar land. Well, except for the time I stumbled across what looked like good-quality roe in a famous New York food emporium. My experience told me that this was a quality product, but its unbelievable price, seven dollars for about a pint, had me confused. I bought it, figuring even that if it was a sham I had nothing to lose. When I tasted it, I recognized it as good domestic sturgeon, comparable to a Caspian sevruga. A couple of days later, I returned to the store to stock up. When I asked the manager about this roe, he was visibly pained. An entire gallon bucket of American sturgeon roe had been mispriced. "Whoever bought that caviar got the deal of a lifetime," he said. I didn't have the heart to tell him. But it goes to show you the value of being an educated consumer.

BEACH PLUM AND FOIE GRAS CANAPÉS

Part of my annual pilgrimage to Cape Cod is stocking up on the local beach plum jelly, made from the small fruits that grow wild by the sea. Too sour to eat raw, the plums make a wonderful tangy jelly that is delicious with foie gras and other game meats. Surprise your guests by concealing the jelly under a smooth blanket of foie gras mousse.

MAKES 24 CANAPÉS

1 tablespoon plus ⅜ teaspoon kosher salt

1 cup very finely shredded Savoy cabbage

¼ teaspoon sugar

2 teaspoons gin

8 thin slices rye bread

6 ounces prepared or homemade foie gras mousse (page 59)

2 tablespoons beach plum or currant jelly

1. Bring a small pot of water to a boil. Add the 1 tablespoon salt, drop in the cabbage, and boil for 2 minutes, or until the cabbage turns a bright green. Drain the cabbage and plunge it into a bowl of ice water. Drain and squeeze the cabbage dry. Season with the ⅜ teaspoon salt, the sugar, and gin. Set aside.

2. Preheat the oven to 350°F. With a cookie cutter about 2 inches long and 1 inch wide, or one 1½ inches in diameter, cut 3 pieces from each slice of bread. Place the cut bread on a baking sheet and toast in the oven for 10 to 12 minutes, or until crisp and lightly browned. Set aside.

3. Soften the mousse or foie gras with a sandwich spreader or wooden spoon until it is spreadable. Mound ¼ teaspoon jelly in the center of each toast. Spread about ½ tablespoon of the mousse or foie gras over the jelly with a sandwich spreader or knife to conceal the jelly completely. Smooth the mousse or foie gras with a knife to make a smooth edge flush with the edge of the toast. Top each canapé with a little of the cabbage and serve.

WHITE-TRUFFLED GRISSINI

After a magnificent November day of truffle hunting outside Alba, my host, Gianmaria Bonino of the venerable truffle brokerage Tartufi Morro, organized a seven-course truffle lunch. One of the many unforgettable elements of that meal was the cheese course. Each guest was served a selection of terrific local cheeses drizzled with olive oil and showered with white truffles. The maitre d' placed a dozen grissini, those long, crisp bread sticks ubiquitous in the Piedmont area of Italy, in the center of the table. Almost ritualistically, my fellow diners broke the grissini into pieces and used them as a foil to the truffled cheese and oil. The contrast of the crisp bread and silky cream with the truffles' woodsy perfume was divine.

Although truffle oil is a not a traditional addition to grissini, it reminds me of that autumn day. I love these with cheese, or snapped into manageable lengths and wrapped with prosciutto, or simply on their own with a glass of wine.

MAKES ABOUT 20 STICKS; SERVES 6 TO 8

¾ cup warm (105°F) water

1 teaspoon active dry yeast

3 tablespoons white truffle oil, plus more for brushing

2 cups all-purpose flour

1½ teaspoons kosher salt

Cornmeal, for dusting

1. Pour the water into the bowl of a heavy-duty mixer and sprinkle the yeast over the surface of the water. Let sit until foamy, about 5 minutes.

(continued on next page)

2. With the machine fitted with the paddle attachment and running on low speed, beat 1 tablespoon of the truffle oil, one-third of the flour, and the salt into the yeast mixture. Add another tablespoon of the oil and then another third of the flour, then the remaining 1 tablespoon truffle oil and enough of the remaining flour to make a soft dough.

3. Switch to the dough hook and knead the dough for 10 minutes at low speed. Brush a medium bowl with truffle oil, add the dough, and cover the bowl with plastic wrap. Let rise in a warm place until tripled in size, 2 to 3 hours.

4. Preheat the oven to 400°F. Turn the dough out onto a work surface and press the dough into a rectangle about 4 by 14 inches. Using a pizza wheel or a knife, cut a cross to divide the dough into 4 pieces. Cut each section of dough into 5 long pieces. Stretch and roll each strip of dough on your work surface with open flat hands into a round stick about 14 inches long. If the dough is sticky, lightly flour your hands, not the work surface. (If the pieces of dough are taut, cover them with a kitchen towel and set aside for 10 minutes before stretching and rolling.)

5. Place the grissini on two cornmeal-dusted baking sheets and brush them with truffle oil. Bake for 20 to 25 minutes, rotating the pans back to front once during baking, or until light brown. Let cool on rack.

In Piedmont, the world-famous White Truffle Festival is held in the city of Alba every October. Started in the 1920s to promote local agriculture and wine, it has grown into an international event. The popularity of the fair and the worldwide connection between Alba and white truffles is so strong that hunters bring their truffles from other regions to sell to Piedmont wholesalers so that their truffles can be branded as coming from Alba.

FOIE GRAS MOUSSE

Making a mousse is a great way to use up small pieces of foie gras. If you want to extend the yield from this recipe, add 4 tablespoons room-temperature butter when creaming the foie gras. If making your own mousse seems daunting, you can buy already prepared mousse (see pages 40–42).

SERVES 4 TO 6

6 ounces grade-B or -C duck foie gras, clean (page 41)

2 tablespoons Cognac, Armagnac, or Sauterne

¾ teaspoon kosher salt

Freshly ground pepper to taste

1 cup chicken stock (page 173)

2 sprigs thyme

2 gratings nutmeg

1 tablespoon minced summer or black winter truffle (optional)

1. Combine the foie gras, brandy or wine, salt, and pepper in a small bowl. Refrigerate for 1 hour.

2. Drain the foie gras marinating liquid into a small saucepan. Add the stock and thyme. Bring to a boil, reduce heat, and simmer for 1 minute to make a poaching broth.

3. Put the foie gras in the hot broth, cover, and turn off the heat. Poach for 5 minutes, or until the foie gras has an internal temperature of 115°F. Remove the foie gras from the broth. Transfer the broth to a small bowl and set over ice to cool it to room temperature. Return the foie gras to the cool liquid and refrigerate for 1 hour.

4. Remove the foie gras from the liquid, pat dry, and puree the foie gras along with any rendered fat in a food processor until smooth. (If the mousse gets a broken, curdy look to it, add about 1 tablespoon of the poaching liquid to stabilize the emulsion.) Taste and adjust the seasoning. Add the nutmeg and truffle, if desired. Transfer the mousse to a ramekin. Refrigerate for 2 to 3 hours before serving.

FIRST COURSES

A well-planned meal should have a deliberate progression, scored so that the foods complement each other, bringing out the best qualities in the ingredients. Serving caviar, foie gras, or truffles as a first course makes for an auspicious beginning of a meal, and many times it is the perfect way to experience a member of this trio. The chilled delicate flavor of Caspian caviar, for example, is best savored when your palate is fresh, and a terrine of foie gras is ideal as the opening act in a special meal. Truffles, which pair up so superbly with risotto and pasta, are customarily served before the main course. Smaller dishes are how most people first enjoy these delicacies.

Don't feel limited to serving the dishes in this chapter only as the prelude to a meal; instead serve two or three together to make an unforgettable event. Or take advantage of the impact caviar, foie gras, and truffle have at the table and make them the center of an elegant meal composed of smaller dishes.

COOL STARTERS

Caspian Caviar with Bianca's Brioche

Smoked Trout and Big Apple Salad with Black Truffle Vinaigrette

Seared Foie Gras, Roasted Pear, and Winter Green Salad

Buckwheat Noodles with Roasted Eggplant and Salmon Caviar

Snapper Carpaccio with a Lemongrass Drizzle and Osetra

Caviar Beggar's Purses

Terrine of Foie Gras with Fall Fruits

Asian-Spiced Foie Gras Torchon with Carrot-Radish Chutney

Caviar and Smoked Sturgeon Sandwiches

Russian Ice-House Soup

Whipped Herb Custard with Sevruga

Salt-Cured Foie Gras with a Frisée Salad

⊙⊙

WARM STARTERS

Champagne-Poached Oysters with Sevruga

Pumpkin Bisque with Foie Gras

Tajarin with Fresh White Truffle

Seared Foie Gras with Sour Cherry Confit

Truffled Vegetable Strudel

Sesame-Crusted Foie Gras with Pomegranate-Glazed Peaches

Wild Mushroom and Truffle Risotto with a Foie Gras Option

Black-Tie Pasta

Fresh White Truffle Risotto

*Rigatoni with Mushrooms, Smoked Ham Hocks,
and Truffled Cheese*

⊙⊙

CASPIAN CAVIAR WITH BIANCA'S BRIOCHE

Whether starring as the centerpiece for an impressive cocktail party or nibbled in bed as an antidote to the stresses of the world, the dark pearls of good caviar are always thrilling. There is much to be said about the ritual of serving caviar, and how you set the stage should reflect your personality. But one thing is true: To really appreciate the nuances of the taste and texture of caviar, serve it as unadulterated as possible.

To make the most of your portion, remove the caviar from the refrigerator about 10 minutes before serving, but do not open the container until right before serving. If you have a caviar presentoir, a dish that holds the caviar in a bed of ice, that's a boon, but it is by no means essential. You can set a very luxurious stage for your caviar by simply placing the container in a bowl of shaved ice. Never transfer caviar from its jar or tin to another dish, because that damages the delicate beads. Display the lid right next to it, not only to indicate the type, but also to enjoy the wonderful design found on many caviar caps. Then, choose your spoon. Caviar reacts with silver, developing a metallic taste, so although elegant, it's the wrong choice for caviar. Homey plastic will do, but tiny mother-of-pearl paddles, or wood, gold, or horn spoons are ideal. (Expert Russian caviar tasters simply put a dollop of the sturgeon's roe in the little hollow in the crook of their hands between the thumb and forefinger and lick it off.)

The question of what to serve with caviar is simple. When you have the best, all you really need is something to drink. Delicate beluga resonates wonderfully with brut Champagne or with its comrade, vodka. As I learned from Scott Skye, the chef at Caviar Russe in New York City, it's fun to experiment with the interplay between beverages and caviar. He introduced me to combining osetra with a quality lighter-style microbrewed beer. Although it doesn't have the cachet of caviar and Champagne, the nuttiness of this species of caviar was excellent with the yeastiness of beer. Skye tastes hundreds of tins of caviar a year, and his drink of choice with briny sevruga is chilled sake. "It brings out the sea in the caviar, reminding you of the parallel between sashimi and caviar," he says. The flavor of caviar changes with what you are drinking. A fun way to experience your caviar is to serve it with various beverages to stimulate different qualities of the caviar's taste.

Eating caviar by the spoonful is not only the stuff of modern-day fairy tales, it's the best way to do it. The culinary cliché of chopped egg, onion, and sour cream is superfluous. Accompaniments should be kept minimal and neutral, to cleanse the palate. The ideal choices are a fine light-grained bread like a white bread or brioche, sliced boiled potatoes, or pancakes like crepes or plain blini. If you want a bit of crème fraîche, that's okay, but don't douse the eggs with it.

BIANCA'S BRIOCHE

MAKES 1 LOAF; SERVES 4 TO 6

SPONGE:

1 package active dry yeast (2¼ teaspoons)

¾ cup lukewarm (100°F) milk

1 cup all-purpose flour

8 tablespoons unsalted butter at room temperature

3 tablespoons sugar

½ teaspoon fine sea salt

2 large eggs, at room temperature

2½ cups all-purpose flour

1 to 3 ounces of caviar per person or as much as your purse allows

(continued on next page)

1. To make the sponge: Sprinkle the yeast over the surface of the milk and let sit undisturbed for a couple of minutes until the granules of yeast plump. Stir to blend. Put 1 cup of flour in a medium bowl. Pour in the yeast mixture and stir with a wooden spoon until smooth, about 1 minute. Cover with plastic wrap and set aside in a warm spot for 30 minutes, or until almost doubled in size.

2. In the bowl of a heavy-duty mixer, beat the butter with the paddle attachment on medium-high for 1 minute, or until smooth, creamy, and light. With the machine running, add 1 tablespoon of the sugar at a time. Add the salt. Stop the machine and scrape down the sides of the bowl with a rubber spatula. With the machine running, add the eggs one at a time, making sure that each is completely incorporated before adding the next. The butter and eggs should be completely smooth and not curdy.

3. Reduce the speed to low and add the 2½ cups flour, mixing until just blended. Stop the machine and scrape down the sides of the bowl again. Add the sponge and mix for about 30 seconds. Turn the machine off and switch to the dough-hook attachment. Knead the dough for 15 minutes on medium-low speed.

4. Butter the inside of a large bowl. Remove the dough from the mixer and form it into a ball. Roll the ball around in the buttered bowl to coat it. Place the dough, seam-side down, in the bowl. Cover the bowl tightly with plastic wrap and let the dough rise in a warm place, until doubled in size, about 1 hour.

5. Butter a 9-by-5-inch loaf pan. Turn the dough out onto a clean work space and press out the air. Knead the dough 3 to 4 times. Press the dough out to form a rectangular piece the length of the loaf pan. Form it into a loaf with a smooth top. Place the loaf, seam-side down, in the pan and cover loosely with plastic wrap. Let rise in a warm place until doubled in size, about 1 hour. The dough should be light, spongy, and feel slightly fragile when touched.

6. Preheat the oven to 375°F. Bake the loaf in the center of the oven for 35 to 40 minutes, or until deeply browned. Remove from the oven and let cool on a wire rack for 10 minutes. Turn the brioche out of the pan and let cool completely before slicing. Serve with the caviar.

The future of the Caspian Sea is in question. The world's largest landlocked sea, it covers 143,000 square miles, is fed primarily by the Volga River in the north, and has no natural outlet. The Caspian is ringed by five distinct countries: Russia, Kazakhstan, Turkmenistan, Azerbaijan, and Iran. Due to environmental degradation, many parts of the sea are severely polluted, particularly the traditional sturgeon spawning areas. Besides man's unfortunate influence on the sea, there has been a natural fluctuation in the sea level since the 1920s. The sturgeon live in the brackish waters of the Caspian, and these factors have affected their natural spawning grounds. The fisheries in the north, historically administered by Russia, also compete with a densely industrial use of the region. The northern Caspian is shallower than the sea off the southern shores of Iran and Azerbaijan. Some experts prefer caviar from the south because of the depth and better quality of the water that the fish spawn in. Finally, vast oil reserves exist under the Caspian, and the drilling and transport of oil threaten the ecology of the sturgeon habitat.

SMOKED TROUT AND BIG APPLE SALAD WITH
BLACK TRUFFLE VINAIGRETTE

*In the fall, New York City's produce markets are brimming with
Hudson Valley apples. Their whimsical names—Winesaps, Ida Reds,
Jonagolds, Crispins, Northern Spys—echo the magic of the orchard. At
the height of the season there can be up to forty different varieties. A
favorite thing I do in my cooking classes is to have a side-by-side tast-
ing of the different apples. Whether tart, juicy, crisp, rich, or floral, it is
always a revelation to realize how each apple variety's taste is unique.
When you experience the different facets of one fruit, you realize how
complex an ingredient can be. When I make this salad, I use a mix of
red, green, and yellow apples for a contrast of taste, texture, and color.*

SERVES 4

3 unpeeled firm, semi-tart apples like Macoun, Northern Spy, or
  Cortland, or a mixture, cored

½ cup crème fraîche

½ cup thinly sliced celery, plus a couple of leaves

2 tablespoons prepared white horseradish, drained

2 tablespoons chopped fresh flat-leaf (Italian) parsley

1 teaspoon fresh thyme leaves

Kosher salt and freshly ground black pepper to taste

1 bunch watercress, stemmed (about 3 cups)

1 large bunch arugula, stemmed (about 3 cups)

Leaves from ½ head red or green Boston lettuce (about 3 cups)

Black Truffle Vinaigrette (recipe follows)

2 smoked trout, boned and skinned

1. Cut the apples into bite-sized pieces. In a small bowl, fold together
the apples, crème fraîche, celery, horseradish, parsley, thyme, salt, and
pepper. Set aside. (Some crème fraîche is very thick; if necessary, thin
it with a little milk so that it coats the fruit.)

2. Just before serving, toss the greens with the vinaigrette. Divide the greens among 4 plates. Place the apple salad in the center of the greens. Flake the trout over the apple salad and serve.

BLACK TRUFFLE VINAIGRETTE

MAKES ABOUT ½ CUP

2 teaspoons Dijon mustard

2 tablespoons white wine vinegar

2 teaspoons minced fresh thyme

1 teaspoon kosher salt

Freshly ground black pepper to taste

6 tablespoons black truffle oil

In a small bowl, combine the mustard, vinegar, thyme, salt, and pepper. Gradually whisk in the truffle oil to make an emulsified dressing.

There can be a huge difference in the quality of truffle oils; some have a strongly artificial, gassy aroma, while others have a balanced perfume that relies on natural flavors. Buy oils in small quantities, since their aroma and flavor does dissipate once opened.

SEARED FOIE GRAS, ROASTED PEAR, AND WINTER GREEN SALAD

Bosc pears can be unmercifully hard, unthinkable to eat out of hand. Roasting transforms them, revealing their veiled, tender sweetness. In these days of packaged salad mixes, it's positively retro to rip, wash, and dry your own greens, but this hardy mix is worth the effort. Peppery watercress, nutty arugula, and crisp escarole provide a wonderful balance to the foie gras and pears. Try this salad, sans foie gras, with a significant blue cheese, like Stilton, Spanish Cabrales, or Gorgonzola.

SERVES 6

3 Bosc pears, peeled, quartered, and cored

2 tablespoons unsalted butter or rendered foie gras fat, melted

¼ teaspoon ground coriander

⅛ teaspoon ground allspice

Kosher salt and freshly ground black pepper to taste

1 red onion

2 teaspoons olive oil

VINAIGRETTE:

2 tablespoons sherry wine vinegar

1 tablespoon Dijon mustard

1 teaspoon kosher salt

Freshly ground black pepper to taste

3 tablespoons walnut oil

5 tablespoons extra-virgin olive oil

6 cups torn escarole leaves

1 bunch watercress, stemmed (about 3 cups)

1 large bunch arugula, stems trimmed (about 3 cups)

**12 to 18 ounces foie gras, cut into 6 medallions, each about
½ inch thick (see page 41)**

Kosher salt and freshly ground black pepper to taste

1. Preheat the oven to 375°F. In a medium bowl, toss the pears with the butter or fat. Sprinkle with the spices, salt, and pepper. Toss to coat the pears evenly. In a large ovenproof skillet over medium heat, sauté the pears until they sizzle, about 4 minutes. Transfer the pears to the oven and roast, turning them a couple times, until golden brown and tender, 25 to 45 minutes. Set aside and keep warm.

2. Meanwhile, cut the onion in half through the root end and then into ½-inch wedges attached at the root. Toss with the olive oil, salt, and pepper. Spread the onions out in a shallow pan and roast in the oven until soft, about 20 minutes.

3. Meanwhile, make the vinaigrette: In a medium bowl, whisk together the vinegar, mustard, salt, and pepper. Gradually whisk in the walnut and olive oils to make a creamy dressing. Set aside.

4. When ready to serve, toss the greens together. Divide the pears and onions among 6 salad plates. Heat a large, heavy skillet over high heat. Season one side of the foie gras medallions with salt and pepper. Place the medallions in the pan, seasoned-side down, and cook for 2 to 3 minutes, or until browned. Drain any excess fat. Season the medallions with salt and pepper, turn the foie gras with a flat spatula, and cook for 1 or 2 more minutes, or until softened but still firm. Transfer to a paper towel to drain briefly. Lightly dress the greens with the vinaigrette and divide among the plates. Top each salad with a medallion of foie gras and serve immediately.

BUCKWHEAT NOODLES WITH ROASTED EGGPLANT AND SALMON CAVIAR

Buckwheat is a natural with the briny-sweet taste of salmon roe and the smoky taste of roasted eggplant. But the surprise is how well eggplant and caviar pair up. When making this salad, don't skip the step of rinsing the noodles, or they will be overly starchy.

SERVES 4

3 Japanese eggplants

Kosher salt to taste

DRESSING:

3 tablespoons rice vinegar

3 tablespoons mirin

1 tablespoon fresh lime juice

2 teaspoons grated peeled fresh ginger

1¼ teaspoons kosher salt

Freshly ground black pepper to taste

¼ cup soy or peanut oil

1 tablespoon Asian sesame oil

8 ounces Japanese buckwheat noodles

2 cups pea shoots, cut into 2-inch lengths

Kosher salt and freshly ground pepper to taste

3 ounces salmon roe

2 tablespoons paper-thin slices scallion tops or snipped fresh chives

1. Preheat the broiler. Prick the eggplant in 5 or 6 spots with a fork. Broil the eggplant as close to the heat source as possible until charred, turning it to blacken it evenly on all sides, about 5 to 7 minutes. (You can also char the eggplant directly over a high gas flame.) Wrap the blackened eggplants in aluminum foil to steam for 5 minutes, or until soft. Let cool. Peel away the charred skin of the eggplant under running water. Pat dry with paper towels. Chop the eggplant, season with salt, and set aside.

2. To make the dressing: In a medium bowl, whisk together the vinegar, mirin, lime juice, ginger, salt, and pepper. Gradually whisk in the two oils to make a smooth dressing. Set aside.

3. Bring a large pot of water to a boil. Add salt. Boil the noodles until just tender, 4 to 5 minutes. Drain and rinse thoroughly with cold running water for 3 to 4 minutes. Shake off the excess water and toss the noodles with the dressing.

4. To serve, toss the noodles with the eggplant and pea shoots. Season with salt and pepper. Divide the salad among bowls and top each one with salmon roe and scallions or chives. Serve immediately.

The finest salmon roe comes from the wild chum salmon of the Pacific Northwest. The eggs should be firm and uniformly round, and the best are an orange-reddish color. The eggs should hold their shape and be refreshingly rich and briny, as well as have a sweet taste. Russian varieties are sold under the name *keta*. Salmon roe is not as perishable as sturgeon caviar, but it should be consumed within a week of purchase.

SNAPPER CARPACCIO WITH
A LEMONGRASS DRIZZLE AND OSETRA

When a fish is impeccably fresh, one of the best ways to experience its sweet sea taste is as carpaccio. When the raw opal-colored slices of snapper are topped with beads of dark caviar, it is a stunning indulgence as well. Complementing the fish with a lemongrass-infused oil and a crisp snow pea and corn salad adds a vibrant taste and texture. Steep the lemongrass oil 1 day ahead. Any surplus oil can be used in Asian-flavored salads or on grilled fish.

SERVES 4

LEMONGRASS OIL:

½ **teaspoon coriander seeds**

Pinch of aniseeds

1 whole stalk lemongrass, coarsely chopped

½ **cup vegetable oil**

1 pound chilled red snapper fillets, pin bones removed

4 ounces snow peas, trimmed and cut into thin diagonal slices

¼ **cup fresh corn kernels, such as Silver Queen**

1 teaspoon rice vinegar

Fine sea salt and freshly ground black pepper to taste

¼ **cup radish sprouts (about ½ ounce)**

1 to 2 ounces osetra caviar

1. To make the lemongrass oil: Crush the seeds in a mortar with a pestle. Add the lemongrass and pound, bruising the stalk. In a small pan, combine the lemongrass mixture with the oil. Cook over medium heat just until the lemongrass begins to sizzle, about 3 minutes. Remove from heat and let cool. Cover and let sit at room temperature overnight. Strain.

(continued on next page)

2. Cut 8 squares of parchment paper, each about 8 inches square. With a very sharp, thin knife, cut the snapper into ⅛-inch-thick pieces by cutting broad, diagonal slices, starting from the head end of the fillet, as you would slice smoked salmon. Lay a quarter of the slices of the snapper on a piece of parchment in a single layer, making a rough circle. Place another piece of parchment on top and, with the flat side of a chef's knife, gently pound the fish into an even layer. Repeat with the remaining fish. Cover and refrigerate until ready to serve.

3. In a small saucepan of salted boiling water, cook the snow peas until they turn a vibrant green, about 30 seconds. Scoop the peas from the water, and transfer to a small bowl of ice water to stop the cooking and set their color. Boil the corn in the same small saucepan of salted boiling water for about 1 minute. Drain and transfer to the bowl of water with the snow peas. Drain the vegetables and blot dry with paper towels. Toss the snow peas and corn with 2 teaspoons of the lemongrass oil, the vinegar, salt, and pepper.

4. To serve, place the sheets of carpaccio on a work surface. Peel off the top piece of parchment and lightly season the fish with salt and pepper. Invert the carpaccio onto individual plates and peel away the parchment so that the carpaccio lies evenly in the center of the plate. Drizzle each portion of fish with about ½ teaspoon lemongrass oil. Toss the sprouts with the snow peas and corn, mound the salad in the center of each carpaccio. Dot the surface of the fish with 4 to 5 small mounds of osetra and serve immediately.

CAVIAR BEGGAR'S PURSES

Caviar beggar's purses—crepe pouches bursting with caviar and crème fraîche—were the signature dish of the Quilted Giraffe. In the high-flying 1980s, when caviar and Champagne flowed in celebration of an ascending Dow, nimble-fingered cooks would tie up hundreds of purses a day. On the first day on the job, young cooks would be presented with an intimidating original tin of Petrossian beluga caviar and a stack of warm crepes. There was very little room for imperfection. A well-made purse is plump, like a little money bag topped off with a ruffle, reminiscent of an Elizabethan collar.

Today, I prefer to use bolder-flavored sevruga or even salmon roe for purses. If tying purses is more work than you're interested in, invite your guests to slather open-faced, warm crepes with crème fraîche.

MAKES 24 PURSES; SERVES 6

CREPES

1½ cups whole milk, at room temperature

4 large eggs

1 cup pastry flour, or ¾ cup all-purpose flour mixed with ¼ cup cake flour

⅛ teaspoon fine sea salt

1 tablespoon unsalted butter melted, plus more for brushing on the pan, if needed

24 to 30 fresh chives

½ cup crème fraîche

6 ounces sevruga caviar, American paddlefish roe, or salmon roe

3 limes, each cut into ⅛-inch slices (24 slices total)

2 tablespoons unsalted butter, warm melted

(continued on next page)

1. To make the crepes: In a medium bowl, whisk the milk and eggs together. Sift the flour and salt into another medium bowl and make a well in the center of the flour. Pour the wet ingredients into the well. Gradually whisk the flour into the wet ingredients, stirring in one direction, to make a smooth batter. Strain the batter through a fine-meshed sieve into a medium bowl, pressing any lumps through. Set the batter aside for 1 hour at room temperature.

2. Heat a well-seasoned or nonstick 5- to 6-inch crepe pan over low to medium-low heat. Stir the melted butter into the batter. Stir the batter gently to even out the consistency. (Do not aerate the batter or the crepes will be lacy.) Lay a sheet of plastic wrap about 14 inches long over a plate.

3. Brush the crepe pan with melted butter. Ladle 2 tablespoons crepe batter into the pan and swirl the pan to cover it with a thin film of batter; pour any excess batter back into the bowl. The first couple of crepes can be tricky if the pan is not at the right temperature. If the pan is too hot, the crepes will be lacy; if too cool, the batter will not adhere to the pan. Cook the crepe on one side only for about 45 seconds, or until the edges curl a bit and there is a very light blush of brown on the underside. Remove the crepe from the pan and lay it on the plastic wrap. Repeat, stacking the crepes. Wrap the crepes in the plastic and set aside until ready to make the purses. (They can be made a day ahead and refrigerated. Bring to room temperature before separating.)

4. Bring a small saucepan of water to a boil. Leave the rubber band on the bunch of chives or tie a string around them, drop them into the boiling water, and cook until the chives are limp, about 30 seconds. Transfer the bundle of chives to a bowl of cold water. Drain the chives and lay them out on a paper towel.

5. Spread 4 crepes out on a work surface. Place 1 teaspoon crème fraîche in the center of each crepe. Top with a heaping teaspoon caviar. To form the purse, lift one edge of the crepe up at the 3 or 9 o'clock position with your dominant hand, and hold the crepe at 12 o'clock between the thumb and forefinger of your other hand, so the bottom of the crepe just touches the work surface. With your dominant hand, fold the edge of the crepe into tight pleats about ¼ inch long, holding the pleats between the forefinger and thumb of the other hand. When the ruffles are formed, the last part of the crepe will enclose the pleats. Press the center of the last bit of crepe into the center of the pleats to open them up into a full ruffle. Hold the purse together and tie it closed with a chive just above the filling, so the purse is a plump package. Trim the chive with a knife or scissors. Cut off the excess floppy crepe so that the ruffle extends ½ inch above the filling. Repeat with remaining crepes and caviar. Serve now or refrigerate until ready to serve.

6. To serve, bring the purses to room temperature, if chilled. Place the lime slices on a serving dish. Place a purse on each lime slice and brush very lightly with the warm butter. Serve immediately.

Note: Some people find it easier to cut the crepes before pleating. At the restaurant, we would cut the crepes into neat 5-inch discs with the cleaned lid of an old 1-pound caviar tin. You may not have a tool like that in your kitchen, but be resourceful and see what you can use. I use the bottom of the tin that holds my cookie cutters.

TERRINE OF FOIE GRAS WITH FALL FRUITS

A terrine of foie gras, classic and elegant, is the purest way to enjoy this delicacy. The key to a successful terrine is removing any unsightly veins or blemishes from the liver and cooking it very gently at a low temperature in a water bath. First-quality grade-A livers are the only choice for terrines, because of their pristine appearance and composition. Making and serving a homemade foie gras terrine is a luxury to be relished by both the cook and his or her guests.

SERVES 8 TO 10

1 grade-A duck foie gras

2 teaspoons kosher salt

3 tablespoons white port or Sauterne

Mulled Italian Plums and/or Gingery Seckel Pears (recipes follow)

1. Let the foie gras sit at room temperature for 1 hour. Separate the larger lobe from the smaller one by gently pulling them apart. Place the smooth side of the foie gras on the counter. Find the spot in the larger lobe where the veins surface. With a small paring knife, pry the foie gras open and follow the major veins into the liver. (The veins form tributaries from a central main core.) Remove the veins from the liver, by pulling gently, using pliers if necessary. Take care not to break up the liver too much. Scrape any red blemishes from the liver. Pat dry with a towel. Repeat with the smaller lobe.

2. Place the liver, smooth-side down, in a bowl or dish just large enough to hold it. Season with salt and white port or Sauterne. Press plastic wrap on the surface of the liver and refrigerate overnight.

3. Preheat the oven to 200°F. Remove the foie gras from the refrigerator 20 minutes before cooking. Place the smaller lobe, smooth-side down, in a small terrine mold. Place any broken bits on top and then cover with the larger lobe, smooth-side up. Press the liver in the mold

(continued on next page)

to make sure it is quite compact. Line a medium roasting pan with paper towels. Place the terrine in the pan and pour hot water halfway up the side of the mold. Cover the mold with a lid or aluminum foil. Bake for 40 minutes, or until a thermometer inserted into the foie gras registers between 115° and 120°F. (Since oven performance varies greatly, check the terrine for doneness after about 30 minutes.) Remove the terrine from the oven and water bath. Let cool at room temperature for 30 minutes.

4. Leaving about ¼ to ½ inch of fat on the surface, pour the excess fat from the terrine and reserve. Cut a piece of Styrofoam or cardboard the size of the opening of the mold and wrap it in plastic wrap. Place it on the surface of the terrine and place a 16-ounce can on top to weight the terrine. Refrigerate for at least 48 hours or up to 1 week.

5. The foie gras can be served from the mold or unmolded. To serve slices, unmold the terrine and trim it if needed. With a warm knife, cut the foie gras into slices. To present it in the terrine, pour some melted reserved fat on the surface and refrigerate until set. Score the surface of the terrine with a knife. Serve the foie gras by scooping it out of the terrine with a warm spoon. If not eating all of the terrine at one time, store it well wrapped in plastic wrap for up to 1 week after cooking. Serve with the drained poached fruit (recipes follow).

MULLED ITALIAN PLUMS

MAKES ABOUT 2 CUPS

1½ cups ruby port

½ cup water

2 tablespoons honey

4 whole cloves

2 peppercorns

½ cinnamon stick

12 ounces Italian plums, peeled

1. In a medium saucepan combine all of the ingredients except the plums. Bring to a simmer and cook over medium heat for 5 minutes.

2. Drop the plums into the spiced liquid, reduce the heat to very low, and poach the plums until tender, 25 to 30 minutes. Do not let the liquid boil, or the fruit will be mushy. Let cool in the liquid and set aside until ready to use.

GINGERY SECKEL PEARS

SERVES 4 TO 6 AS A GARNISH

1½ cups white verjus (available at specialty foods stores)

½ cup honey

4 slices fresh ginger

6 allspice berries

8 seckel pears (about 8 ounces) peeled, stems intact

1. In a medium saucepan, combine all of the ingredients except the pears. Bring to a boil, cover, reduce heat to low, and cook for 5 minutes.

2. Drop the pears into the spiced liquid. Reduce the heat to very low and poach the fruit until tender and not mushy, about 30 minutes. Be careful not to boil the pears. Set aside and let cool in the liquid.

ASIAN-SPICED FOIE GRAS TORCHON WITH CARROT-RADISH CHUTNEY

Foie gras torchons—a whole liver or a single lobe, twisted up in a cloth to a party-favor shape, then poached—have become very popular with chefs lately. This preparation allows for a sleek, round shape to slice and present, and gives the cook more opportunities to accent the flavor of the liver than a standard terrine. Be aware that when you remove the liver from the broth it will be flabby and should be handled gently, but it will set up in a matter of hours in the refrigerator.

SERVES 6

1 large lobe grade-A duck foie gras, about 1 pound

3 teaspoons kosher salt

½ teaspoon sugar

2 cups white port

8 slices fresh ginger

1 teaspoon coriander seeds

½ teaspoon fennel seeds

½ teaspoon allspice berries

7 cups chicken stock (page 173)

Carrot-Radish Chutney for serving (recipe follows)

1. Let the foie gras sit at room temperature for 1 hour. Place the smooth side of the foie gras on a work surface. Find the spot in the lobe where the internal veins surface. With a small paring knife, pry the foie gras open around the vein and follow the major veins into the liver. (The veins form tributaries from a central main core.) Remove the veins from the liver by pulling gently, using pliers if necessary. Take care not to break up the liver too much. Scrape any red blemishes from the liver. If necessary, rinse the liver with cool water and pat it dry with a towel.

2. Season each side of the liver with 1 teaspoon of the salt and the sugar. Cut a piece of cheesecloth about 12 by 16 inches and spread it out on a work surface with the shorter end facing you. Place the lobe, smooth-side down and parallel to the short edge, on the lower third of the cheesecloth. (Place any small pieces of foie gras on the thinner part of the liver to make an even thickness.) Starting with the shorter end, roll the cheesecloth around the foie gras to form a tight fire-crackerlike shape. Mold the foie gras as needed to form an even cylinder. Twist the ends of the cheesecloth to compress the liver as much as you can to form a very tight package. Tie off the ends with string or strips of cheesecloth. Wrap in plastic wrap and refrigerate for at least 6 hours or overnight.

3. In a large saucepan, combine the port, ginger, and spices. Bring to a boil, reduce heat, and simmer for 5 minutes. Add the stock and remaining salt. Cover, reduce heat to very low, and simmer for 30 minutes. Strain into a deep skillet or other pan just large enough to accommodate the torchon when added. Bring to a simmer.

4. Lower the torchon into the poaching liquid and turn off the heat. Cut a circle of parchment paper to fit on the surface of the stock. (This will control the temperature of the poaching liquid and keep the torchon from floating above the surface.) Poach the torchon for 15 minutes. Hold the torchon by the ends of the cheesecloth and carefully transfer it to a plate. The foie gras will be very delicate at this point, so handle it gently. Let cool to room temperature, then refrigerate until firm, about 2 hours. Remove the cheesecloth and reroll the torchon in a fresh piece of cheesecloth. Twist the torchon into a compact, uniform, sausagelike shape. Refrigerate for 2 days.

5. To serve, remove the torchon from the cheesecloth. Slice the torchon into ½- to ¾-inch rounds. Serve with the Carrot-Radish Chutney.

(continued on next page)

CARROT-RADISH CHUTNEY

One of the greatest joys of teaching is learning from your students. Samia Ahad, a former student and a very talented cook, introduced me to the nuances and sophisticated tastes of her native South Asian cuisine. This carrot chutney is inspired by the wonderful flavors she has shared with me. Toasting the black mustard seeds enhances their flavor and perfumes the oil that coats the carrots.

SERVES 4 TO 6 AS A GARNISH

1½ teaspoons black mustard seeds (available at Indian markets)

1 whole clove

3 tablespoons peanut, corn, or other vegetable oil

1½ teaspoons grated peeled fresh ginger

2 cups julienned carrots

2 tablespoons water

¼ teaspoon kosher salt

1 tablespoon fresh lemon juice

Pinch of cayenne pepper

1½ ounces 2-inch-long daikon sprouts

1. In a medium skillet over medium-high heat, cook the mustard seeds and clove in the oil until the seeds lighten in color and pop, about 1 minute. Add the ginger and cook, stirring, until lightly browned, about 30 seconds. Add the carrots, water, and salt. Stir to combine evenly, cover, and steam until the carrots soften slightly and lose their raw taste, about 1 minute. Transfer the carrots to a bowl, add the lemon juice, and let cool.

2. Add the cayenne and daikon sprouts. Taste and adjust the seasoning. Remove the clove and serve. This can be made up to 2 hours ahead.

CAVIAR AND SMOKED STURGEON SANDWICHES

In Vladimir Nabokov's Speak Memory, *he describes his father's exodus from revolutionary Russia:*

> . . . my father followed a dim corridor, saw an open door
> at the end, walked onto a side street and made his way to
> the Crimea with a knapsack he had ordered his valet Osip
> to bring to a secluded corner and a package of caviar sand-
> wiches which good Nickolay Andreevich, our cook, had
> added of his own accord.

You don't need to be on the run to appreciate the restorative powers of sturgeon. Set a crock of the butter out with the bread, fish, and tin of caviar and let your guests enjoy making these open-faced sandwiches themselves.

SERVES 4

½ cup (1 stick) unsalted butter at room temperature

½ teaspoon grated lemon zest

¼ teaspoon ground black pepper

¼ teaspoon vodka

8 to 12 slices pumpernickel bread

8 ounces thinly sliced smoked sturgeon

3 to 6 ounces sevruga caviar or pressed caviar

1. In a small bowl, cream together the butter, lemon zest, pepper, and vodka. Use now or cover and refrigerate for up to 24 hours. Remove from the refrigerator 30 minutes before serving so that the butter will spread easily.

2. To serve, spread each slice of bread with the butter, top with a bit of the sturgeon, and finish with as much caviar as your purse will allow.

RUSSIAN ICE-HOUSE SOUP

This Chlodnick, a Russian soup—adapted from a recipe by Michael Field—is sublimely simple and refreshing. Its surprising ingredients, buttermilk and sauerkraut juice, provide a balanced, cool backdrop for the cucumber, shrimp, and festive roe. If you aren't a Russian with a vat of sauerkraut to siphon off the needed juice, or you don't have quality fresh kraut to drain, bottled juice can be purchased at a natural foods store. This soup also makes a neat amuse *served in demitasse cups.*

SERVES 6

1 cucumber, peeled, seeded, and diced

1½ teaspoons kosher salt, plus salt to taste

2½ cups buttermilk

1¼ cups sour cream

⅓ cup fresh sauerkraut juice

1 small garlic clove

2 tablespoons minced fresh dill, plus sprigs for poaching and garnish

⅓ cup finely chopped fennel bulb

1 scallion, including green parts, finely chopped

Freshly ground white pepper to taste

SHRIMP:

1½ cups water

1 teaspoon fennel seeds

¼ teaspoon coriander seeds

1 scallion, including green parts, chopped

6 fresh dill sprigs

½ teaspoon white peppercorns

8 ounces medium or large shrimp in the shell

3 ounces lumpfish roe (red, orange, or a mixture) rinsed and dried, for garnish

1. Put the cucumber dice in a colander and rub them with 1 teaspoon of the salt. Set aside in the sink for 30 minutes to drain and crisp.

2. In a large bowl, whisk the buttermilk, sour cream, and sauerkraut juice together until smooth. Use the flat side of a chef's knife to smash the garlic clove with ½ teaspoon of the salt into a smooth puree; add this to the soup. Stir in the dill, fennel, scallion, and cucumber. Season the soup with salt and pepper. Cover and refrigerate for 4 hours.

3. Meanwhile, poach the shrimp: In a small saucepan combine the water, fennel seeds, coriander seeds, scallion, dill sprigs, and peppercorns. Bring to a simmer over low heat and cook covered for 5 minutes. Add the shrimp and cook uncovered over low heat until they curl and turn pink, about 3 minutes. Drain and let cool. Shell the shrimp and split them in half lengthwise along the vein. Remove the vein.

4. Pour the soup into chilled shallow soup bowls. Scatter the shrimp over the top and garnish with a dollop of caviar and sprigs of dill.

There are endless stories in the caviar business of shady salesmen showing up unannounced at the back door of restaurants or retail shops with black suitcases full of tins of caviar to sell for a song. Be assured that this is not a product anyone wants; beyond the likelihood that caviar of this pedigree would be smuggled or illegal or just old, it is unrefrigerated and refrigeration is an absolute necessity for sustaining caviar. Old caviar will break down and lose its texture, becoming either dry or excessively runny as the eggs collapse and develop white protein deposits.

WHIPPED HERB CUSTARD WITH SEVRUGA

Eggs and caviar is a time-honored combination. This custard is whipped over a pan of simmering water in a matter of minutes, like a sabayon. The resulting custard is a perfect pillow for the sevruga. Do this ahead and all you need to do at party time is dollop on the caviar.

SERVES 6

½ cup heavy cream

6 large egg yolks

2 tablespoons dry white vermouth

½ teaspoon kosher salt

Freshly ground black pepper to taste

1 teaspoon thinly sliced fresh chives

1 teaspoon minced fresh tarragon

1 teaspoon minced fresh chervil

1 teaspoon minced fresh flat-leaf parsley

1.7 to 3 ounces sevruga caviar

1. In a deep bowl, beat the cream until soft peaks form. Cover and refrigerate.

2. In a medium stainless-steel or ceramic bowl, beat the egg yolks, vermouth, salt, and pepper together until foamy and light, about 1 minute. Set the bowl over a pan of barely simmering water and beat with an electric mixer or whisk until the eggs thicken, about 2 minutes. (Keep the mixer moving around in the eggs as they are cooking so the edges don't curdle. If the eggs are setting too quickly, lift the bowl from the pan and whisk the mixture off heat before returning it to the heat.)

3. Remove from the heat and continue to whisk until the mixture is cooled to room temperature, about 1 minute. Fold the cream and herbs into the egg. Divide the custard among 6 small custard or espresso cups. Refrigerate for 2 hours. Top each custard with caviar and serve.

SALT-CURED FOIE GRAS WITH A FRISÉE SALAD

This is an easy and interesting way to cook foie gras, because it doesn't heat the liver at all. Instead, the liver is buried in salt for 2 days, which firms it and concentrates its flavor. If I have bought a whole liver and sautéed half of it, I like to do this with the leftover lobe of foie gras.

SERVES 6

6 to 8 ounces grade-A or -B foie gras, in one piece

Approximately 6 cups kosher salt

Frisée Salad (recipe follows)

1. Let the foie gras sit at room temperature, for 1 hour. Clean as you would the terrine, page 80.

2. Cut a piece of cheesecloth about 12 by 10 inches and spread it out on a work surface with a short end facing you. Place the foie gras, smooth-side down, parallel to the edge facing you on the lower third of the cheesecloth. Start to roll the cheesecloth around the foie gras to form a tight firecrackerlike shape. Twist the ends of the cheese-cloth to compress the liver as much as you can to form a tight package. Tie off the ends with string or strips of cheesecloth.

3. Pour one-third of the salt into a ceramic loaf pan or terrine. Set the liver in the salt and pour the remaining salt over it to bury it completely. Refrigerate for 24 hours.

4. After 24 hours, remove the foie gras log and break up the salt. Return the liver to the salt and refrigerate for another 24 hours.

5. When ready to serve, remove the liver from the salt and cheese-cloth. Slice the foie gras very thinly or shave it into curls with a peeler. Divide the salad among 6 plates. Set a slice or several curls of the cured foie gras on each toast and garnish the salads with them. Serve immediately.

FRISÉE SALAD

VINAIGRETTE:

2 tablespoons balsamic vinegar

1 tablespoon whole-grain mustard

½ teaspoon kosher salt

Freshly ground black pepper to taste

6 tablespoons extra-virgin olive oil or black truffle oil

6 to 8 slices multigrain bread

Leaves from 1 head frisée (about 8 cups)

1 large bunch watercress or arugula, stems trimmed (about 3 cups)

1 endive, cut into thin diagonal slices

1. To make the vinaigrette: In a medium bowl, whisk together the vinegar, mustard, salt, and pepper. Gradually whisk in the olive oil or black truffle oil to make a creamy dressing.

2. Toast the bread and cut each slice into 4 triangles. Toss the greens with the dressing.

In the Age of Enlightenment, as French society became democratized, foie gras found its apogee in the famous pâté de Strasbourg, an elaborate construction of a whole foie gras wrapped in forcemeat and baked inside a pastry crust. Jewish farmers in Alsace are credited with producing the finest livers for this dish.

CHAMPAGNE-POACHED OYSTERS WITH SEVRUGA

Serving Champagne, oysters, and caviar together is a gustatory grand slam. If your guests are true fans, the added effort of opening the oysters yourself will be appreciated. The advantage of taking this task on is that you won't lose any of the their bracing liquor, which is the foundation for the sauce. If this operation is daunting, a good fish store should be happy to pop the bivalves for you, but remember to ask them to save the juices.

SERVES 4

20 medium oysters, such as Wellfleets or Blue Points, scrubbed

1 cup flat brut Champagne

¼ cup dry white vermouth

1 tablespoon minced shallot

1½ cups heavy cream (preferably not ultra-pasteurized)

Freshly ground black pepper to taste

1 to 2 ounces Caspian sevruga or American caviar

1. To open the oysters: Lay the rounded shell of the oyster on a folded towel on a work space; angle the hinge of the shell toward you. Drape another towel around your hand for protection and place it on the oyster to hold it still. Insert an oyster knife or an old-fashioned church-key can opener into the hinge where the 2 shells come together. Gently rock the knife or opener up and down until the shell pops free. (Oysters open by leverage, not force.) Hold the open oyster over a small bowl so as to not lose any of the liquor. Run a sharp knife along the top and bottom of the shells to release the oyster, then put it in the bowl with the oyster liquor. Repeat with the remaining oysters. Refrigerate for up to 6 hours until ready to cook.

2. Clean the curved oyster shells and divide them among 4 indented oyster plates or other rimmed plates.

3. Combine the Champagne, vermouth, and shallot in a medium saucepan. Carefully pour the reserved oyster liquor, but not the oysters, into the wine. Place the pan over medium heat, bring to a boil, and simmer for 8 to 10 minutes, or until the liquid is reduced by three-fourths. Add the cream and simmer until reduced by about a third, or until it forms viscous bubbles and coats the back of a spoon. Season lightly with pepper. Use now or set aside for up to 2 hours.

4. To serve, reheat the sauce to just under a simmer, if necessary. Slide the oysters into the sauce and poach them over low heat for about 2 minutes, or until they are heated through, plumped, and their edges just begin to ruffle. Spoon the oysters into the prepared shells with the sauce. With a plastic or other nonreactive spoon, place a dollop of caviar on each oyster and serve immediately.

Interestingly, the consumption of both sturgeon and its roe is not allowed by two dominant religions of the eastern Mediterranean, Islam and Judaism. The dietary practices of both of these religions forbid the eating of this fish, since it does not have scales. It was a sin to even touch the fish, which ultimately led to the leasing of the fishing grounds off the Iranian shores of the Caspian to Russian merchants and dealers. Iranian-owned participation in the caviar trade has really been only a twentieth-century phenomenon. The last Shah was famous for his love of caviar, serving only the finest and rarest. After his overthrow and the ensuing political conflict between the United States and Iran, an embargo was placed on Iranian caviar; this was lifted in 2000.

PUMPKIN BISQUE WITH FOIE GRAS

Both truffles and foie gras have a natural affinity for pumpkin. There are elaborate ways to enjoy these flavors, such as in ravioli or by baking a whole foie gras tucked inside a squash. One of the simplest preparations, however, a straightforward soup, is my favorite. When the earthy orange flesh of the squash is blended to a silky bisque and finished off with foie gras, it gives new meaning to "great pumpkin." Use any leftover soup as a sauce with gnocchi or pasta.

SERVES 6 TO 8

4 tablespoons unsalted butter

2 leeks, including light green parts, sliced and thoroughly rinsed

2 garlic cloves, smashed

2½ pounds diced peeled pumpkin or other winter squash, such as Hubbard, red kuri, or kabocha (about 8 cups)

1 bay leaf

1 teaspoon fresh thyme leaves

2 fresh sage leaves

8 cups chicken stock (page 173) or water

1 tablespoon kosher salt

Freshly ground black pepper to taste

3 tablespoons Armagnac or brandy

4 slices light whole wheat bread, crusts trimmed, cut into triangles

2 teaspoons white truffle oil

3 to 4 ounces prepared or homemade duck or goose foie gras terrine (page 80) or mousse (page 59)

1. In a medium soup pot, melt the butter over medium heat. Add the leeks and garlic, cover, and cook for 10 minutes, or until softened. Add the pumpkin, herbs, and stock and bring to a boil. Season with the salt and pepper. Reduce heat to low, cover, and cook for 20 minutes, or until the pumpkin is completely tender.

(continued on next page)

2. Remove the bay leaf and sage. Puree the soup with a handheld immersion blender or in batches in a blender. Return the soup to the pot and add the Armagnac or brandy. Bring the soup to a simmer. Taste and adjust the seasoning.

3. To serve, preheat the broiler. Place the bread triangles on a small baking sheet and toast about 6 inches from the heat, turning to brown both sides. Drizzle the warm toasts with the truffle oil. Dice the foie gras terrine or scoop the mousse and divide it among warmed shallow soup bowls. Pour soup into bowls and serve immediately, with the truffle toasts.

TAJARIN WITH FRESH WHITE TRUFFLE

Tajarin are the unforgettable fresh egg-yolk-rich noodles of the Piedmont region of Italy, the heart of white truffle country. The noodles, which are almost saffron yellow due to the farmhouse yolks, are the customary accompaniment to fresh white truffles. There is a culinary bravura to recipes for tajarin, which can max out with up to 40 egg yolks per kilo of flour. Making handmade noodles is definitely a commitment, but when you are slicing fresh white truffles, it is worth the effort.

SERVES 6 TO 8

3½ cups unbleached all-purpose flour

2 teaspoons kosher salt, plus more salt to taste

4 large eggs at room temperature

8 large egg yolks at room temperature

Fine cornmeal for dusting

12 tablespoons (1½ sticks) unsalted butter, diced

1 cup chicken stock (page 173)

2 to 4 tablespoons freshly grated Parmigiano-Reggiano cheese

Freshly ground black pepper to taste

2 ounces fresh white truffle

1. Mound the flour and the 2 teaspoons salt on a clean work space and make a well in the center. Crack the whole eggs into the well and add the egg yolks. Break up the eggs and yolks with a fork and gradually combine them with the flour by stirring bits of flour into the well with the fork. Use your other hand to move the flour around to keep the eggs from running out of the flour. (It is like moving the walls of a sand castle to keep the water inside.) Keep mixing the flour into the eggs until all the eggs have been absorbed and you have a rough dough. Knead the dough until smooth and satiny, about 10 minutes. Wrap the dough in plastic and set aside for 1 hour at room temperature. Do not refrigerate the dough, or it becomes pasty.

(continued on next page)

2. Divide the dough into 6 pieces and cover with a towel. Flatten a piece with a rolling pin into a rectangle that will fit through the widest setting of a pasta machine. Feed the dough through the machine, then fold the flattened dough like a business letter. Pass the folded dough through the machine again. Repeat until the dough is satiny smooth, 3 to 4 times. Close the machine's rollers down by 1 notch and feed the dough through the machine. Repeat this at each setting down to the next-to-last setting. To prevent the dough from scrunching up in the rollers, pull lightly on the part of the dough feeding into the rollers to keep an even tension. (If the dough gets too long to pass through easily, cut the piece in half.)

Lay the sheet of pasta out to dry on a large towel or tablecloth. Roll the rest of the dough. Let the dough dry slightly until it is not tacky but is still pliable, about 20 minutes. (If the dough gets too dry, it will not cut properly.)

3. Cut the dough into foot-long pieces. Pass the sheets through the tagliatelle cutters of the pasta machine. Dust the pasta with cornmeal and twist it into nests. Set on a rack to dry for at least 1 hour and up to 12 hours.

4. When ready to serve, bring a large pot of water to a boil and salt it liberally. Add the pasta and stir to prevent clumps. Cook at a rapid boil until the pasta is al dente, 2 to 5 minutes, depending on how long the pasta has been drying.

5. Meanwhile, in a Dutch oven or large skillet, whisk 6 tablespoons of the butter with the chicken stock over low heat. Drain the pasta and toss in the pan with the remaining 6 tablespoons butter and the cheese. Season with salt and pepper to taste. Divide the pasta among 6 to 8 warmed shallow bowls. Serve immediately. Shave paper-thin slices of truffles over the pasta at the table.

SEARED FOIE GRAS WITH SOUR CHERRY CONFIT

This was the way I first learned to cook foie gras. Like many cooks, I was intimidated by the mystique of these special livers. After a couple of passes with them, I realized that they are very easy to cook. Bring the foie gras to room temperature 10 minutes before cooking to assure even cooking. Foie gras is different from other proteins, however, which firm as they cook. Foie, because of its gras—French for fat—softens. Overcook foie gras and it will render all its fat and liquefy.

SERVES 4

SOUR CHERRY CONFIT:

1 cup dry red wine, preferably Pinot Noir or Zinfandel

3 coin-sized slices fresh ginger

1-inch piece cinnamon stick

¼ teaspoon fennel seeds, cracked

6 allspice berries

4 black peppercorns

12 ounces fresh sour cherries, stemmed and pitted, or thawed
frozen sour cherries

3 tablespoons sugar

1 teaspoon arrowroot mixed with 1 teaspoon water

¼ teaspoon kosher salt

4 medallions grade-A or -B foie gras, 3 to 4 ounces each (see page 41)

Kosher salt and freshly ground black pepper to taste

2 cups mixed salad greens or torn escarole leaves

1. To make the confit: In a medium saucepan, combine the wine, ginger, cinnamon, fennel seeds, allspice, and peppercorns. Bring to a boil, reduce heat to a simmer, and cook to reduce to about ¼ cup.

Meanwhile, combine the cherries with the sugar in a small bowl and let sit to macerate.

2. Add the cherries and juice to the wine reduction. Bring to a simmer and cook just until the fruit is covered by the juice. Whisk the arrowroot mixture into the cherries and bring to a boil. Season with the salt and set aside. (The confit can be made a day or two ahead and refrigerated.)

3. To serve, divide the cherry confit among 4 warmed plates. Season the foie medallions with salt and pepper. Heat a large, heavy bottomed skillet over high heat. Add the medallions to the pan and cook for 2 to 3 minutes, or until deep brown. Turn the foie gras with a metal spatula and cook for 2 to 3 minutes more, or until the foie gras softens but still has some resilience. Drain off any excess fat. Transfer the foie gras to paper towels to drain briefly. Turn the heat off and toss the greens in the pan to wilt slightly. Place the greens and foie gras on the plates and serve immediately.

TRUFFLED VEGETABLE STRUDEL

The filling for this strudel is a blend of winter's pearly roots: turnips, celery root, and leeks. Lowly turnips usually don't get center stage, but when cast with truffles they deserve a starring role. If working with phyllo is unnerving, remember that the key is to have everything ready and organized before you open the package and to work confidently. Handling phyllo is like riding a horse: If you are timid it will take full advantage, but if you take control it will follow your lead.

SERVES 4

1 cup quartered peeled baby turnips or diced peeled large turnips

1 cup diced peeled celery root

1 leek, white part only, sliced and rinsed

5 ounces small button or cremini mushrooms, trimmed and quartered

½ cup dry white wine

1 cup water

3 tablespoons unsalted butter

3 tablespoons prepared or homemade truffle butter (page 175)

1 teaspoon kosher salt, plus salt to taste

Freshly ground black pepper to taste

¾ cup heavy cream

2 tablespoons, plus 1 teaspoon dried bread crumbs

6 sheets room temperature phyllo dough

1½ tablespoons ground toasted blanched almonds (see page 46)

3 tablespoons canned black truffle juice

4 fresh flat-leaf parsley sprigs

1. In a medium saucepan, combine the vegetables, wine, water, 1 tablespoon of each butter, the 1 teaspoon salt, and the pepper. Bring to a gentle simmer and cook until tender, about 12 minutes. Using a slotted spoon, transfer the vegetables to a medium bowl.

2. Bring the liquid to a boil and cook to reduce it by two-thirds. Add ¼ cup of the cream, bring to a boil, and cook until thickened slightly. Add ¼ cup of the sauce to the vegetables along with the 2 tablespoons bread crumbs. Season with salt and pepper to taste. Set the remaining sauce aside while you make the strudel.

3. To make the strudel: Preheat oven to 400°F. In a small saucepan, melt all of the remaining butters together. Skim off the foamy white milk solids and add it to the vegetables. Reserve the clear butter.

On a work surface, place an 18-inch-long piece of parchment paper with a long side facing you. Cover it with 1 sheet of the phyllo, brush the phyllo lightly with some of the butter, and dust with some of the almonds. Repeat with 5 more sheets of the phyllo. (Save a little butter for brushing the outside of the strudel.) On the final sheet, sprinkle the remaining 1 teaspoon bread crumbs to absorb any excess moisture while cooking.

Mound the vegetable mixture evenly along the long side facing you, leaving a 2-inch border at each end. Using the parchment paper as a guide, roll the strudel tightly. Turn it seam-side down and fold the ends under to enclose the filling. Transfer the strudel, by lifting the parchment, to a baking sheet. Brush the strudel with butter and bake in the center of the oven for 25 to 35 minutes, or until golden. Set the pan on a wire rack and let the strudel cool to warm. (The strudel may be made a couple of hours in advance and kept at room temperature. Reheat in a preheated 200°F oven for 10 minutes.)

4. Meanwhile, finish the sauce: Add the remaining ½ cup cream and the truffle juice to the sauce and bring to a boil. Simmer over medium heat until the sauce lightly coats a spoon. Season to taste with salt and pepper.

5. To serve, cut the strudel into 8 equal pieces. Divide the sauce among warmed plates and place 2 pieces of the strudel on each plate, cut-side up. Garnish with parsley sprigs and serve immediately.

SESAME-CRUSTED FOIE GRAS WITH
POMEGRANATE-GLAZED PEACHES

Sesame seeds provide a crunchy contrast to the silken texture of foie gras and add a Middle Eastern touch. Traditional flavors of the eastern Mediterranean, such as pomegranate molasses, aromatic spices, and onions blended with sumac, all are a wonderful complement to foie gras. Sumac is a purply-red berry that is ground to a powder and used in Lebanese cooking for its lemony taste. Although only a small amount of the spice blend called baharat *is called for here, make a full batch. (Like sumac, it is also available commercially.) With a batch of baharat, the sumac, and a bottle of the pomegranate molasses in your pantry, you'll have the beginnings of other terrific Middle Eastern meals.*

SERVES 4

½ onion, sliced into paper-thin rounds

½ teaspoon kosher salt, plus salt to taste

2 teaspoons ground sumac (available in Middle Eastern and spice markets)

1 tablespoon minced fresh flat-leaf parsley

1 tablespoon minced fresh mint

1 tablespoon pomegranate molasses

1 tablespoon water

4 unpeeled ripe peaches, halved and pitted

4 teaspoons extra-virgin olive oil

½ teaspoon Baharat Spice Blend (recipe follows)

¼ cup raw sesame seeds

4 medallions grade-A or -B foie gras, 3 to 4 ounces each (see page 41)

Freshly ground black pepper to taste

(continued on next page)

1. Rub the onion slices with the ½ teaspoon salt and set aside in a small bowl for 10 minutes to soften. Rinse the salt off the slices and pat dry with paper towels. Mix the onion with the sumac, parsley, and mint. Set aside.

2. Preheat the broiler. Mix the pomegranate molasses with the water and set aside.

3. Brush the peaches all over with the olive oil and place on a small ovenproof pan, cut-side up. Sprinkle the peaches with the baharat. Turn the peaches over again and broil them 4 to 5 inches from the heat source until the skin blisters and blackens a bit, 3 to 4 minutes. Turn the peaches over and broil the second side until lightly browned, 1 to 2 minutes. Brush the peaches lightly with some of the pomegranate molasses mixture. Return to the broiler for about 1 minute, or until browned. (Watch the peaches, because the pomegranate molasses can burn easily.) Remove the peaches from the broiler. Let cool and pour the cooking juices from the fruit into the pomegranate molasses.

4. Put the sesame seeds in a pie tin or on a plate. Season one side of each foie gras medallion with salt and pepper to taste. Press the seasoned side of the foie gras into the seeds to crust one side.

5. To serve, divide the peaches and onions among 4 warmed plates. Heat a large, heavy skillet over medium-high heat. Place the medallions of foie gras in the pan, crusted-side down, and cook until the sesame seeds are lightly browned, about 2 minutes. Season the medallions with salt and pepper. Turn with a flat spatula and cook for 2 to 3 minutes, or until the foie gras softens but still has some resilience. Drain any excess fat. Transfer the medallions to a paper towel to drain briefly. Place the medallions on the plates and drizzle with the reserved pomegranate mixture. Serve immediately.

BAHARAT SPICE BLEND

MAKES ABOUT 2 TABLESPOONS

½ **teaspoon whole cloves**

½ **teaspoon black peppercorns**

1 teaspoon cumin seeds

2 teaspoons coriander seeds

2 teaspoons sweet Hungarian paprika

2-inch piece cinnamon

Seeds from 6 green cardamom pods

In a spice mill or mortar, combine the ingredients and grind to a powder. Store in a tightly sealed jar.

WILD MUSHROOM AND TRUFFLE RISOTTO WITH A FOIE GRAS OPTION

The first time I ate risotto was an epiphany. I was working at Hubert's restaurant, and a fellow cook, Nina Fraas, had just returned from Italy and wanted to share with the staff the wonderful flavors she had experienced abroad. The resulting wild mushroom risotto was fantastic. I couldn't believe that anything could taste that good. I persuaded Nina to teach me the secret to her risotto. Years later, I still hear her as I move a flat-bottomed wooden spoon in figure eights through the rice and into the corners of the pan, so the risotto cooks evenly.

SERVES 4

5 to 6 cups chicken stock (page 173)

8 ounces shiitakes or other wild mushrooms, stemmed and quartered (reserve stems)

2 tablespoons unsalted butter

1 shallot, minced

1½ teaspoons kosher salt

1¾ cups Arborio rice

½ cup dry white wine

⅓ cup (3 ounces) canned black truffle juice

2 tablespoons truffle butter (page 175)

⅓ cup freshly grated Parmigiano-Reggiano cheese, or 3 tablespoons prepared or homemade foie gras mousse (page 59)

Freshly ground black pepper to taste

1. In a medium saucepan combine the stock and mushroom stems and bring to a low simmer.

2. In a Dutch oven or large, heavy saucepan, melt the unsalted butter over medium-high heat. Add the shallot and sauté until translucent, about 1 minute. Add the mushrooms and sauté until wilted and lightly browned, about 4 minutes. Season the mushrooms with ¾ teaspoon of

the salt. Add the rice and stir with a wooden spoon until the rice is mixed with the mushrooms, lightly coated with butter, and opaque. Pour the white wine into the pan and stir until all the wine has been absorbed by the rice and the browned bits on the bottom of the pan have melted into the liquid. Pour in the truffle juice and ½ cup of the stock. Stir the liquid until it is absorbed into the rice.

3. Continue adding the stock, about ½ cup at a time, stirring until each addition is absorbed completely into the rice before adding more liquid. (Give the pan a shake periodically to keep the level of the rice even in the broth.) It takes about 20 minutes for the rice to absorb the stock. The finished risotto should be creamy, not loose or gummy, and the center of the grains of rice al dente, but not chalky. When the rice is almost done, add the truffle butter and cheese or foie gras and the remaining ¾ teaspoon salt. Stir vigorously to make sure that they are thoroughly incorporated and creamy. Adjust the consistency with the stock or water. Season with salt and pepper. Let the risotto sit for 1 minute, then ladle into warmed shallow bowls and serve immediately.

TRUFFLED RISOTTO FRITTERS:

Leftover risotto is a boon, if you know how to handle it right. When you have goodies like truffles in it, you don't want that risotto to languish in your refrigerator. Simply reheated risotto is a gummy shadow of its former self, but formed into spheres and deep-fried, it makes terrific croquettes to enjoy with cocktails or to garnish a salad. Form the cold leftover risotto into 2-tablespoon-sized balls. Dip the balls in lightly beaten egg and roll in fresh bread crumbs. Pour 3 inches of oil into a heavy pot. Heat the oil to 350°F and fry the croquettes until golden brown, about 3 minutes. Using a slotted spoon, transfer to paper towels, drain, and serve.

BLACK-TIE PASTA

The hardest thing about this dish is paying for the caviar, but doing so is well worth it. When I serve this, my happy guests literally wipe their bowls clean.

SERVES 4

2 cups very small cauliflower florets (each about ½ inch wide)

8 ounces bow-tie pasta

⅓ to ½ cup crème fraîche, at room temperature

2 tablespoons minced fresh chives

2 to 3 ounces sevruga caviar

Freshly ground black pepper to taste

1. In a medium saucepan of salted boiling water, cook the cauliflower until tender but firm, about 5 minutes. Drain and rinse under cold water to stop the cooking.

2. In a large pot of salted boiling water, cook the pasta until just al dente, about 10 minutes. Drop the cauliflower into the pot with the pasta and cook until heated through, about 30 seconds. Drain the pasta and cauliflower in a colander, leaving a little of the cooking water clinging to the pasta. Transfer to a large bowl. Toss the pasta and cauliflower thoroughly with the crème fraîche and chives. Add the caviar and pepper and toss lightly. Divide the pasta among 4 warmed shallow bowls and serve immediately

FRESH WHITE TRUFFLE RISOTTO

When truffles hit their peak in mid-November, it's time for this excep-
tional risotto. To make a risotto for pairing with fresh white truffles,
the broth needs to be flavorful, but not overly gelatinous. I poach a
whole chicken with vegetables to get the right balance of flavor.
Although it may seem indulgent to poach a whole bird just for the
broth, the truffles warrant that level of respect. The process of making
the broth is a joyful part of this autumn ritual, and the chicken can be
used in a salad with a truffle vinaigrette.

After you have gone through all the steps to make the risotto, enjoy the
ceremony of serving it. Call your guests to the table as you finish the
risotto, and pass the truffle around so they can experience the immediacy
of its untamed aroma. Then serve the risotto and let each guest slice the
truffle over his or her bowl of rice.

SERVES 6

BROTH:
1 tablespoon olive oil

1 stalk celery, sliced

2 carrots, peeled and sliced

1 onion, sliced

2 cloves garlic, smashed

One 3- to 4-pound free-range organic chicken, giblets reserved

10 cups water

2 sprigs thyme

3 sprigs flat-leaf parsley

1 bay leaf

⅛ ounce dried porcini mushrooms

4 teaspoons kosher salt

6 tablespoons unsalted butter

¼ cup minced shallots

2 cups Arborio rice

⅓ cup grated Parmigiano-Reggiano cheese

1½ to 2 ounces fresh white truffle

1. To make the broth: In a medium stockpot over medium heat, heat the oil and sauté the vegetables and garlic, stirring frequently, until tender, 5 to 7 minutes. Reserve the liver for other dishes. Add the giblets to the stockpot and cook for 3 to 5 minutes.

2. Truss the bird by tying the legs together and folding the wing tips on the back of the bird. Add the water and chicken to the pot along with the thyme, parsley, bay leaf, and porcini. Bring the water to a boil. Skim off any foam. Reduce heat to very low and poach the chicken for 1 hour. Remove the chicken from the pot and reserve for another dish. Remove any surface fat and scum from the broth. Bring the broth to a gentle boil and cook to reduce to 6 or 7 cups. Strain and season with the salt. (This can be made up to 3 days before and refrigerated.)

3. In a large saucepan, bring the broth to a simmer over medium heat. In a large, heavy saucepan, melt 2 tablespoons of the butter over medium heat and sauté the shallots until translucent, 2 to 3 minutes. Add the rice and stir with a wooden spoon until the grains are coated. Ladle 1 cup of the broth into the rice and stir until it is absorbed.

4. Continue adding the broth, about ½ cup at a time, stirring constantly as it is absorbed into the rice. This takes approximately 20 minutes for the rice to absorb the broth. The finished risotto should be creamy, but not loose or gummy, and the center of the grains of rice should be al dente, but not chalky. When the rice is just about done, add the remaining butter and cheese and stir vigorously to incorporate them. Adjust the consistency with broth or water. Taste and adjust the seasoning. Let the risotto sit for 1 minute, then ladle into warmed shallow bowls. Shower each bowl with tissue-paper-thin slices of white truffles at the table.

RIGATONI WITH MUSHROOMS, SMOKED HAM HOCKS, AND TRUFFLED CHEESE

This rustic dish is the perfect thing to have simmering on the stove on a wintery Sunday. The ham hocks don't contribute much meat, but their smoky flavor more than makes up for it. One of the rewards of making this is the fantastic rush of truffle aroma when the cheese hits the pasta.

SERVES 6 TO 8

4 ham hocks

3 tablespoons extra-virgin olive oil

2 leeks, including green parts, sliced and rinsed

1 tablespoon minced fresh sage

1½ cups diced butternut squash or other winter squash

2 garlic cloves, minced

12 ounces mixed mushrooms, such as stemmed shiitakes, cremini, and portobellos, diced

Kosher salt and freshly ground black pepper to taste

½ cup dry white wine

1 pound rigatoni pasta

2 cups (8 ounces) shredded sottocenere al tartufo cheese

2 tablespoons minced fresh flat-leaf parsley

1. To purge the hocks of excess salt and smoke, put them in a pot with cold water to cover and bring the water to a boil. Drain and discard the liquid. Cover the hocks with water again and bring just to a simmer over low heat. Cover and poach for 2½ to 3 hours, or until the meat is tender and pulls easily from the bone. Let cool in the broth.

2. Spoon off and discard the fat that has risen to the top of the broth. Reserve 1 cup of the broth. Strip the skin and fat from the bones and separate out the morsels of meat. Reserve 1 tablespoon of the internal fat and discard the rest of the fat. (Save the skin for cooking with beans later, if desired.)

3. Bring a large pot of water to a boil for cooking the pasta. Set the hock meat in a large bowl by the stove. In a large skillet over high heat, heat 1 tablespoon of the olive oil and sauté the leeks until bright green, about 2 minutes. Add ½ cup of the reserved broth and the sage; simmer for 1 minute. Transfer the leeks to the bowl with the ham hock meat.

4. In the same skillet over medium heat, heat 1 tablespoon of the olive oil and the reserved fat from the ham hocks. Add the squash and sauté until tender and lightly browned, about 4 minutes. Add the garlic, and sauté for 1 minute. Using a slotted spoon, transfer the squash to the bowl of leeks.

5. Add the remaining 1 tablespoon oil to the skillet and sauté the mushrooms over high heat until lightly browned and wilted, about 4 minutes. Season with salt and pepper to taste. Add the white wine, and stir to scrape up the browned bits on the bottom of the pan. Cook to reduce the liquid by half. Add the mushrooms to the squash mixture and stir to combine thoroughly.

6. Salt the pasta water generously. Add the pasta and cook until al dente, about 10 minutes. Meanwhile, in a large pot, heat the hocks and vegetables over medium heat. Drain the pasta and toss with the cheese. Add the pasta to the vegetables with the remaining ½ cup broth and the parsley. Toss and heat the pasta over medium heat until the cheese melts, about 2 minutes. Season with salt and pepper to taste. Transfer to a warmed pasta bowl and serve immediately.

MAIN COURSES

Sharing a meal we have cooked is one of the finest ways to express our relationships. We celebrate, comfort, nurture, seduce, and impress through the meals we serve. And no foods make a grander gesture at the table than caviar, truffles, and foie gras.

When you place any one of these ingredients at the center of your meal, it becomes a feast. Generally, we savor these foods in restaurants, an undeniable luxury. But to cook with these ingredients in your own home is to really experience them. Preparing Chicken in Mourning enveloped by the heady aroma of a fresh truffle, or roasting a whole foie gras, or sensually spooning a trio of caviars to serve with hot buckwheat popovers—these are things home chefs dream about. Holding these amazing ingredients in your hands gives you a consummate appreciation for these foods.

This collection of dishes reflects the view that it is best to handle caviar, foie gras, and truffles with restraint. Because of their distinctive qualities and tastes, they don't need overwrought recipes to make them shine. Prepare simple recipes like Steamed Lobster with Truffle Beurre Fondue or Chicken with Riesling—a variation on coq au vin, finished with a swirl of foie gras—and you will see these classics in a new light. These recipes also show the versatility of this trinity to suit a variety of occasions. Serve the Buckwheat Popovers with a Trio of Caviars and Crème Fraîche for brunch, or the Seared Tuna with Tobiko and Avocado for a summer supper, and when you need a showstopper, revel in the preparation of Squab with Black Truffle and Foie Gras. These are dishes that honor the sharing of a meal.

Whole Roasted Truffle for One

Buckwheat Popovers with a Trio of Caviars and Crème Fraîche

Sautéed Veal Chops with Truffled Tomatoes and Arugula

Truffle-Stuffed Salmon with Cabbage

Seared Tuna with Tobiko and Avocado

Poached Fillet of Sole with Smoked Salmon and Caviar

Steamed Lobster with Truffle Beurre Fondue

*Grilled Foie Gras and French Lentil Salad
with Caraway and Roasted Beets*

Chicken with Riesling

Chicken in Mourning

Clay-Baked Pork Roast with Truffled Lentils

Squab with Black Truffle and Foie Gras

Grilled Porterhouse Steak with Summer Truffle

Sautéed Magret with Ginger and Black Pepper Foie Gras Sauce

Medallions of Beef with Foie Gras and Truffles

Whole Roasted Foie Gras with Winter Vegetables

WHOLE ROASTED TRUFFLE FOR ONE

My introduction to truffles was not eating them, but reading the prose of the grand dame of sensual pleasure, Colette. In Earthly Paradise, *she shares her wisdom on truffles: "Away with all this slicing, this dicing and this grating, this peeling of truffles! Can they not love it for itself? If you do love it, pay its ransom royally—or keep away from it altogether. But once having bought it, eat it on its own, scented and grainy skinned, eat it like the vegetable it is, hot and served in magnificent quantities." I take Colette's advice to heart. Although one truffle isn't a lot, it is unquestionably the height of any meal.*

Black winter truffles can be cooked in the oven or tucked among the embers of a glowing fire. Either way, bring your treasure to the table, unwrap it, and savor its full aroma. Eat the truffle paired with a flute of Champagne and toast your fortune and the gifts of nature.

SERVES 1

1 teaspoon unsalted butter at room temperature

1 fresh black winter truffle, 1½ to 2 ounces

Sea salt to taste

2 slices pancetta

3 tablespoons veal (page 173) or chicken stock (page 173)

1 tablespoon aged Cognac or Armagnac

1. Preheat the oven to 400°F. Cut a square piece of aluminum foil and coat it with the butter. Season the truffle with salt. Wrap the truffle in the pancetta and place it in the center of the foil. Draw the foil up into a pouch. Pour the stock and the Cognac or Armagnac over the truffle. Fold the foil closed to make a sealed bundle. Place on a pie plate and roast the truffle for 30 minutes, or until tender.

2. Transfer the truffle to a small plate, along with its cooking juices. Serve immediately and eat with a knife and fork.

BUCKWHEAT POPOVERS WITH
A TRIO OF CAVIARS AND CRÈME FRAÎCHE

For many, a stack of yeasty buckwheat blini is the only accompaniment for caviar. When I want the taste of buckwheat, I pull out my popover pans and whip up this batter. Popovers are great for brunch or impromptu entertaining, because there is no waiting for yeast to rise or having to be anchored at the stove flipping pancakes. You can sit down with your guests and enjoy warm popovers smeared with caviar. Heating the milk and butter before baking assures an impressive puff. These are also delicious with a smear of foie gras and a bit of truffle butter.

MAKES 12 MINI OR 6 LARGE POPOVERS;
SERVES 6

1¼ cups milk

3 tablespoons unsalted butter

1 cup bread flour (not bread machine flour)

¼ cup buckwheat flour

¼ teaspoon fine sea salt

3 large eggs at room temperature

2 tablespoons shortening or lard, or 1 tablespoon *each* melted butter and oil

2 ounces salmon roe

2 ounces golden whitefish roe

2 ounces American sturgeon caviar

1 cup crème fraîche

1. Preheat the oven to 450°F for large popovers and 425°F for mini popovers. Place the oven rack in the center of the oven. Place a nonstick or well-seasoned popover pan in the oven to heat. Put the milk and butter in a saucepan and heat over medium-low to melt the butter. Remove from heat and set aside.

(continued on next page)

2. Sift the flours and salt together into a medium bowl. Whisk the milk mixture into the flour. Beat in the eggs one at a time, whisking well after each addition. Set aside.

3. Carefully remove the pan from the oven and add about ½ teaspoon shortening, lard, or melted butter and oil to each cup. Return the pan to the oven to heat for 3 to 4 minutes. Remove the pan from the oven and divide the batter among the cups. Bake for 20 minutes. Without opening the oven door, reduce the oven temperature to 350°F and bake 15 to 20 minutes longer, or until browned. Remove the popovers from the oven and poke each with a knife to release steam. Serve immediately with the caviars and crème fraîche.

The Convention on International Trade in Endangered Species, or CITES (pronounced SIGHT-ease), initiated strict controls in 1998 to protect all sturgeon and paddlefish. This agreement, signed by all sturgeon-producing and importing nations, changed the way caviar and sturgeon products are traded and set annual limits on the catch of each species of fish. Today, all caviar comes with papers that validate its legal origins and is subject to DNA testing to assure its authenticity. Although these efforts have stabilized quality in the caviar trade industry, we are still years away from a secure sturgeon population, and illegal poaching and smuggling continue to have a serious impact.

SAUTÉED VEAL CHOPS WITH
TRUFFLED TOMATOES AND ARUGULA

Serving a memorable meal without a lot of effort has become a mantra of the twenty-first century. This tomato salad spooned over veal or pork chops has become my failsafe, particularly when I want to put together an impromptu romantic dinner for my husband and myself.

SERVES 2

1½ cups cherry or grape tomatoes, halved

2 tablespoons white truffle olive oil

1 teaspoon white wine vinegar

1 clove garlic, smashed

½ teaspoon kosher salt, plus salt to taste

Freshly ground black pepper to taste

2 loin veal chops, about 1½ inches thick (1½ pounds)

2 tablespoons virgin olive oil

1 bunch arugula, stemmed (about 2½ cups)

1. In a medium bowl, combine the tomatoes, truffle oil, vinegar, garlic, the ½ teaspoon salt, and the pepper. Set aside.

2. Preheat the oven to 400°F. Dry the chops with a paper towel and season one side with salt and pepper to taste. In a large skillet over high heat, heat the olive oil, add the chops, salted-side down, and sauté for 3 minutes, or until brown. Reduce heat to medium and cook for 2 minutes. Season the other side of the veal with salt and pepper to taste and turn. Cook for 5 more minutes, or until browned. Transfer the chops to a roasting pan. Roast in the oven for 5 minutes. Remove the chops from the oven and let them rest at room temperature for about 2 minutes.

3. To serve, divide the arugula between 2 warmed plates. Slice half of each chop and place the chop on the greens with the slices fanned open. Add any collected juices from the veal to the tomatoes and spoon them over the veal. Serve immediately.

TRUFFLE-STUFFED SALMON WITH CABBAGE

Of all the wonderful fish and black truffle combinations, this one is my favorite. Noble salmon, with its rich, assertive taste, stands up to the profound flavor of truffles. Besides being incredibly delicious, the contrast of the pink flesh with the black of the truffles is very beautiful. If you feel uneasy about cutting the pocket in the salmon fillet, ask your fishmonger to do it for you.

SERVES 4

1½ pounds center cut salmon fillet, skin and pin bones removed

½ ounce fresh black winter truffle

1 tablespoon unsalted butter, thinly sliced

Kosher salt to taste, plus 1 teaspoon

2 ounces pancetta, cut into ¾-by-¼-inch pieces

1 small head savoy cabbage (1¼ pounds), cored and thinly sliced

¾ cup water

2 tablespoons Cognac or brandy

1 tablespoon whole-grain mustard

Freshly ground black pepper to taste

1 to 2 tablespoons vegetable or soy oil

1. Lay the fillet on a work surface. Starting from a cut edge of the fillet, use a slicing knife or boning knife to make a large pocket in the fish. Slice the truffle paper-thin with a truffle slicer, mandoline, or a very sharp knife. Tuck the slices into the pocket so they completely cover the inside of the fillet. Dot the inside with the butter slices and season with salt. Wrap the fish in plastic wrap and refrigerate for at least 1 hour or up to 6 hours.

2. To cook the cabbage: In a medium, heavy saucepan over medium heat, sauté the pancetta for 3 to 4 minutes. Add the cabbage and the 1 teaspoon salt. Stir until the cabbage wilts, about 3 minutes. Reduce the heat to medium-low, add the water, cover, and cook for 20 minutes. Add the Cognac or brandy and mustard. Uncover and simmer for 3 to 4 minutes to reduce the excess liquid. Set aside.

3. Remove the salmon from the refrigerator 20 minutes before cooking. Season the rounded side of the salmon with salt and pepper to taste. Heat a large, heavy skillet over medium-high heat. Pour the oil into the skillet and lay the salmon, seasoned-side down, in the pan. Increase the heat to high and cook the fish for 2 minutes. Shake the fish loose, reduce the heat to medium-high, and cook the fish until browned, about 5 minutes. Season the other side of the fish with salt and pepper to taste. Using a wide metal spatula, flip the fish over. Cook the fish for 4 minutes, or until slightly translucent in the center. Transfer the fish to a cutting board and let rest for 2 to 3 minutes.

4. Reheat the cabbage. Using a slicing knife, cut the fillet into 4 square portions so that each has a nifty amount of truffles. Make a bed of cabbage on each of 4 warmed plates or a platter. Put the fish on top and serve immediately.

SEARED TUNA WITH TOBIKO AND AVOCADO

This dish was inspired by the refreshing mixture of rich and crisp flavors found in a tuna sushi roll. Searing the tuna in one large piece over a strong heat rewards you with a golden brown crust and a rosy, buttery interior. The mint and basil in the avocado salad are a cooling foil to the crunchy flying fish roe. Serve the tuna with a fragrant Asian rice for a true inside-out sushi combination.

SERVES 4 TO 6

3 medium Kirby cucumbers, seeded and diced

2 scallions, including green parts, thinly sliced

3 tablespoons minced fresh mint, plus sprigs for garnish

3 tablespoons minced fresh basil

1 teaspoon grated peeled fresh ginger

2 tablespoons seasoned rice vinegar

2 ripe Hass avocados

1 teaspoon kosher salt, plus more to taste

Freshly ground black pepper to taste

One 2-pound sushi-grade tuna steak, 1½ to 2 inches thick, at room temperature

2 tablespoons vegetable oil

2 ounces tobiko (flying fish roe)

1. In a medium bowl, mix together the cucumbers, scallions, mint, basil, and ginger. Dress with the rice vinegar.

2. Cut the avocados in half lengthwise and divide in two. Remove the pit by knocking the blade of a chef's knife into the pit and lifting it from the avocado. With a paring knife, make 4 to 5 lengthwise and 4 to 5 crosswise slices in one avocado half to make a gridlike pattern. With a large spoon, scoop halfway down and across the avocado and

(continued on next page)

then down again to the skin to get evenly diced pieces. Repeat with the other avocado half. Gently fold the diced avocado into the cucumber mixture and season with the 1 teaspoon of salt and the pepper. Set aside.

3. Dry the tuna with a paper towel and season one side of the tuna with salt and pepper to taste. In a large, heavy skillet over medium-high, heat the oil. Add the tuna, seasoned-side down, increase the heat to high, and cook the tuna undisturbed until a rich, golden brown crust forms, 3 to 5 minutes. Season the fish with salt and pepper, turn it over, and sear for 3 to 4 minutes on the other side. Transfer the fish to a cutting board and let rest while you finish the salad.

4. Fold the tobiko into the salad, taking care not to overmix it. Taste and adjust the seasoning. Divide the salad among serving plates. With a sharp knife, cut the tuna into large cubes or slices, place it with the salad, garnish with mint sprigs, and serve.

POACHED FILLET OF SOLE
WITH SMOKED SALMON AND CAVIAR

This is a classic presentation of paupiettes, *or rolled sole fillets, enriched with slices of smoked salmon. The fish is finished off with a caviar butter sauce. Serve with Champagne, so you won't need to open a bottle just for the 2 tablespoons needed for making the sauce. Add the caviar to the sauce right before you serve it, to avoid cooking the delicate eggs.*

SERVES 4

4 fillets of sole (about 1¼ pounds total)

4 ounces thinly sliced smoked salmon

Freshly ground black pepper to taste

2 teaspoons unsalted butter

COURT BOUILLON:

3 cups water

1 cup dry white vermouth or dry white wine

1 onion sliced or 1 leek including light green parts, sliced and rinsed

1 carrot, sliced

1 stalk celery, sliced

1 large sprig flat-leaf parsley

1 large sprig thyme

1 teaspoon kosher salt

CAVIAR BUTTER SAUCE:

2 tablespoons dry Champagne

2 tablespoons crème fraîche

6 tablespoons, cold unsalted butter, diced

1 to 2 ounces sevruga caviar

Kosher salt and freshly ground black pepper to taste

(continued on next page)

1. Cut each fillet in half lengthwise along the natural seam and remove any small bones. Lay each fillet half, skin-side up (the side with a herringbone pattern on it). Place a strip of smoked salmon down the center of each half, leaving a 1-inch margin at the top, or wide end, of the fish. Grind a bit of pepper over the salmon and dot with a few small pieces of butter. Roll the fillets up, starting with the small end. Secure each roll with a toothpick. Lightly butter a sauté pan or gratin dish. Place the rolls in the pan. Cut a piece of parchment paper to fit over the pan and refrigerate.

2. In a medium saucepan, combine all the ingredients for the court bouillon. Bring to a boil, reduce the heat to a simmer, cover, and cook for 20 minutes. Remove and discard the vegetables. (The dish can be prepared 1 day ahead up to this point, and refrigerated.)

3. To poach the fish: Remove the fish from the refrigerator 20 minutes before poaching. Bring the court bouillon just to a boil and pour it into the pan with the sole. Cover with the parchment paper. Poach the fish over low heat until firm but not flaky, about 10 minutes. If the fish rolls are not completely covered by the liquid, turn them over about three-fourths of the way during cooking to cook evenly.

4. Meanwhile, make the sauce. In a small saucepan, cook the Champagne over medium heat until reduced slightly. Add the crème fraîche and heat for 1 minute. Reduce heat to low and whisk a couple of pieces of the butter into the reduction until it melts into a creamy liquid. Continue adding the butter a little bit at a time, whisking until each addition is creamy. (The key is not to let the butter get either too hot or too cold. If it is too hot, it will become oily and separate; if too cold, it will be whipped softened butter, not a sauce. Move the pan on and off the heat if necessary.) Keep warm in a double boiler.

5. Using a slotted spoon, remove the sole from the court bouillon. Remove the toothpicks. Place the fish on 4 warmed plates. Add the caviar to the sauce and season with salt and pepper to taste. Spoon the sauce over the fish and serve immediately.

STEAMED LOBSTER WITH TRUFFLE BEURRE FONDUE

Lobster and black truffles are heavenly together, and many fine restaurants serve this wonderful combination. The lobster, however, is rarely served in the shell, which is too sloppy a presentation for elegantly clad diners and too understated for the average chef. Generally, the lobster is partially cooked, and the meat is pulled from the shell and reheated at service time. When I brought these methods to my home kitchen, this manipulation was too labor-intensive, and I missed the pure taste of freshly steamed lobster.

When I serve lobsters with truffles, simplicity rules. I make a beurre fondue (butter warmed and whisked back into a creamy state), add truffles, and splash this sauce on the freshly steamed lobster meat for an ultimate taste of the sea and earth. Eating the lobster may be a little messy, but that kind of participation with food is one of the great things about cooking and eating together at home.

SERVES 4

½ cup (1 stick) unsalted butter, diced

¾ to 1 ounce fresh black winter truffle

1½ tablespoons water

1 tablespoon canned truffle juice (optional)

½ teaspoon kosher salt

Four 1¼-pound lobsters

1. Put the butter in an airtight container with the truffle and refrigerate for 2 hours or overnight.

2. In a small saucepan, heat the water over medium heat. Whisk a couple of pieces of the butter into the water until it melts into a creamy liquid. Continue adding the butter, a little bit at a time, whisking until each addition is creamy. (The key is not to let the butter get either too hot or too cold. If it is too hot it will get oily and separate;

(continued on next page)

if too cold it will be whipped softened butter, not a sauce.) Add the truffle juice, if using, and the salt. Slice the truffles as thin as you can with a truffle slicer, mandoline, or very sharp knife, and add to the sauce. Put the sauce in a double boiler over warm water to keep warm, as well as to soften the truffle and perfume the sauce.

3. Pour 2 inches of water into a pot that will accommodate all the lobsters, and set up a collapsible steamer. Bring the water to a boil over high heat. Add the lobsters to the pot, cover, and steam for 10 minutes.

4. Remove the lobsters from the pot and split each lengthwise with a heavy knife. To ease the removal of the claw meat, hold the tip of a claw and position it so that it is perpendicular to the work surface. Use a cleaver or the bolster end of a chef's knife to whack a ½-inch notch into the center part of the edge of the large part of the claw. Twist the knife to make a clean crack in the shell, making it easier to remove the meat in one satisfying piece. Repeat with the remaining claws.

5. Divide the lobster among 4 plates and spoon some of the truffle butter over the tail meat. (Make sure that you include pieces of truffle.) Divide the rest of the butter among 4 small bowls. Serve the lobster immediately, with the bowls of butter and with small forks or picks for recovering all the small nuggets of lobster in the shell.

There is a common misconception that truffles should be stored in Arborio rice, and that the rice should then be used for risotto. This does neither the truffle nor the rice any favors. The rice actually dries the truffle out, drawing its aroma from it, and the rice doesn't really retain the perfume.

GRILLED FOIE GRAS AND FRENCH LENTIL SALAD WITH CARAWAY AND ROASTED BEETS

An earthy lentil salad studded with ruby beets is a perfect foil to the smoky richness of grilled foie gras. The salad is tossed with a mustardy caraway vinaigrette, reminiscent of Hungarian traditions with foie gras. For an unforgettable mixed grill, add some grilled duck sausages, smoked pork chops, and whole roasted carrots tossed with rendered foie gras fat.

SERVES 4

2 beets (about 4 ounces total), stalks trimmed to ½ inch

½ small to medium onion

2 whole cloves

⅔ cup green French lentils (lentilles du Puy), picked over and washed

3 cups water

1 small carrot, halved

½ stalk celery, cut into thirds

1 bay leaf

1¼ teaspoons kosher salt, plus salt to taste

4 teaspoons sherry wine vinegar

1½ tablespoons whole-grain mustard

2 teaspoons caraway seeds, toasted and cracked (recipe follows)

1 clove garlic, minced

Freshly ground black pepper to taste

¼ cup extra-virgin olive oil

2 tablespoons minced fresh flat-leaf parsley

Four 4-ounce grade-A or -B foie gras medallions (see page 41)

2 cups mixed salad greens

1. Preheat the oven to 375°F. Wrap the beets in aluminum foil, put them on a small pan, and roast in the oven for 30 to 40 minutes, or until tender when pierced with a knife. Set aside and let cool.

2. Stud the onion with the cloves. In a medium saucepan, combine the lentils, water, onion, carrot, celery, bay leaf, and ¾ teaspoon of the salt. Bring to a boil and cook for 5 minutes. Reduce heat to a simmer and cook until the lentils are tender but hold their shape, 25 to 30 minutes. Drain and discard the vegetables.

3. Meanwhile, make a vinaigrette by combining the sherry wine vinegar in a bowl with the mustard, caraway seeds, garlic, remaining ½ teaspoon salt, and the pepper. Gradually whisk in the olive oil to make an emulsified sauce. Toss the warm lentils with the vinaigrette.

4. Peel the beets by rubbing the skins off with a paper towel. Dice the beets. Stir the beets and parsley into the lentils. Adjust the seasoning.

5. To serve, heat a grill pan over medium heat for at least 2 minutes. Season one side of the foie gras medallions with salt and pepper. Increase heat to high, place the medallions, seasoned-side down, on the grill pan and sear for 2 to 3 minutes. Turn the medallions with a metal spatula and cook for 2 more minutes, or until the foie gras softens but still has some resilience. Transfer the medallions to a paper towel to drain briefly.

6. To serve, divide the greens and lentils among warmed plates, top with the grilled foie gras, and serve immediately.

TOASTING AND CRACKING CARAWAY SEEDS:

In a small, heavy skillet over medium-high heat, toast the seeds, stirring frequently, until fragrant and lightly browned, 3 to 4 minutes. Let cool. Crack in a mortar to release their flavor.

CHICKEN WITH RIESLING

This variation on coq au vin, finished with foie gras mousse, is a great way to give a chicken dinner a little finesse and to use up the last bit of foie gras mousse. Baking the chicken covered with parchment paper keeps the meat tender. Serve this with Truffle-Glazed Parsnips with Onions and Chestnuts (page 168) for a wonderful winter meal.

SERVES 4

One 3- to 4-pound free-range organic chicken, backbone removed, cut into 8 serving pieces

Kosher salt and freshly ground black pepper to taste

1½ tablespoons vegetable oil

Flour for dredging

2 tablespoons unsalted butter

1 onion, sliced

1 carrot, sliced

1 stalk celery, sliced

4 to 6 sprigs thyme

1 bay leaf

4 parsley stems

1 bottle Riesling wine (about 3 cups)

8 ounces cremini or button mushrooms, quartered

1½ cups chicken stock (page 173)

¼ cup heavy cream

¼ cup prepared or homemade foie gras mousse (page 59)

2 tablespoons minced fresh flat-leaf parsley

1. Preheat the oven to 350°F. Season the chicken with salt and pepper. In a large ovenproof skillet or Dutch oven over medium heat, heat the oil. Dredge the chicken in flour and place, skin-side down, in the pan. Add 1 tablespoon of the butter to the pan and sauté the

chicken until golden brown on both sides but not cooked through, about 7 minutes. Transfer the chicken to a plate.

2. Add the onion, carrot, and celery to the pan drippings and sauté until browned, about 5 minutes. Drain any excess fat from the pan. Tie the thyme, bay leaf, and parsley stems together with a string and add to the pan.

3. Pour the wine into the pan and cook over high heat, stirring to scrape up any browned bits from the bottom of the pan. Season with salt and pepper to taste. Return the chicken to the pan, skin-side up. Cut a piece of parchment paper into a circle the size of the pan. Crunch the paper up and wet it with water, then unfold and place it on top of the chicken. Put the pan in the oven and bake the chicken for 30 to 40 minutes or until firm to the touch and cooked through but still tender.

4. Meanwhile, in a medium skillet, melt the remaining 1 tablespoon butter over medium-high heat and sauté the mushrooms until lightly browned, about 5 minutes. Season with salt and pepper to taste. Remove the chicken from the pan and add to the pan with the mushrooms. Keep warm while you make the sauce.

5. To make the sauce: Cook the seasoned wine over medium-high heat to reduce to about 1 cup. Add the chicken stock and cook to reduce again by half, or until slightly thickened. Whisk the cream into the sauce and bring it to a boil. Whisk the foie gras mousse into the sauce but do not boil. Taste and adjust the seasoning. Strain the sauce over the chicken and mushrooms. Cook to heat through, 4 to 5 minutes. Add the parsley and serve.

CHICKEN IN MOURNING

In France, when a chicken is veiled with slices of black truffles under the skin of the breast, it is honored as poulet en demi-deuil, *or half-mourning. But there is no cause for sorrow here, for when a quality bird is dignified in this way it is one of the most delicious means of savoring a truffle's essence. There is a trick, however, to laying the black disks of fresh truffles into an elegant pattern on the bird: Lift the skin away from the meat when you tuck the truffle in, so the slices don't touch the skin until they are in place. The slices are like butterfly wings: Once they touch a moist surface, you can't move them without breaking them up. Place the disks in an overlapping pattern on the meat, then lay the skin on top. Bake the bird in a high-sided pan to keep moisture in and avoid overbrowning the skin.*

SERVES 3 TO 4

One 4-pound free-range organic chicken

1 fresh black winter truffle (about 1½ ounces)

3 tablespoons unsalted butter

Kosher salt and freshly ground black pepper to taste

⅓ cup dry white wine

½ cup chicken stock (page 173)

½ cup crème fraîche

¼ cup canned black truffle juice

1 teaspoon Cognac or brandy

1. Place the chicken on a work surface with the body cavity towards you. Remove the giblets and the large piece of fat at the opening, if present. Slice the truffle paper-thin with a truffle slicer, mandoline, or a very sharp knife. Slip your fingers under the breast skin and carefully loosen the skin from the meat; take care not to tear the skin.

(continued on next page)

Slip the rounds of truffles onto the meat of the chicken breast so they overlap slightly and cover as much of the breast as you can reach from that end. Carefully pull the skin away from the leg and thigh and place truffles on the dark meat as well, tucking a slice or two on the inside of the thighs. Turn the bird around and, working from the neck end, lift the skin and overlap truffles to completely cover the breast. (If you have successfully covered the bird and have truffles slices left, reserve them for the sauce.) Slice 1½ tablespoons of the butter into thin pieces and tuck them under the breast skin on top of the truffles. Mix the remaining 1½ tablespoons butter with any small bits of truffle pieces and refrigerate.

2. Cut the wing tips from the bird and reserve for making stock. Truss the bird with a piece of butcher twine about 3 times the length of the bird. Working with the legs pointing towards you, slip the string under the bird so the center of the string lies right under the middle of the bird, above the legs. Holding the ends of the string, pull the ends along the breasts and slip the string around the wings to pull them snugly against the body of the bird. The string will now be directed toward the tail of the bird and along the breast. Cross the strings at the tip of the breast and pull tightly to compact the bird. Pick up the leg ends with the string and cross them. Turn the bird over, pick up the tail with the strings, and tie off the ends of the twine. Wrap the chicken in plastic and refrigerate for 8 hours or overnight.

3. Remove the chicken from the refrigerator 30 minutes before cooking. Preheat the oven to 400°F. Melt the truffled butter and brush the bird all over with the butter. Season with salt and pepper. Place the bird in a Dutch oven or high-sided ovenproof casserole. Bake in the oven, basting 2 to 3 times with the pan drippings, for 1 hour, or until a meat thermometer inserted in the thigh registers 165° to 170°F. Transfer the bird to a plate and let rest in a warm spot for 10 minutes before slicing.

4. Make a sauce from the pan drippings: Skim the surface fat from the pan drippings or pour the drippings into a degreasing cup and return the pan juices to the pan. Add the wine to the pan and bring to a boil over high heat, stirring to scrape up any browned bits from the bottom of the pan. Cook to reduce the liquid by half. Add the chicken stock and reduce by half. Whisk in the crème fraîche, truffle juice, and Cognac. Simmer until the sauce lightly coats a spoon. Season the sauce with salt and pepper to taste.

5. To serve, remove each side of the breast in one piece, then slice the breast into medallions so that each piece has skin and truffle. Transfer the meat to a serving platter and fan the meat out. Cut the wings, legs, and thighs from the body and arrange them attractively on the platter. Add all the collected juices from the bird to the sauce and bring to a simmer. Taste and adjust the seasoning. Add the sauce to the platter. Serve immediately.

One can't help but be awed by the skill and patience that it takes a truffle hunter to unearth a single truffle, and the way the hunter and his dog know and respect the land. These hunters are the caretakers of the woods. I met one young hunter in Umbria who was keen on protecting truffle lands from environmental degradation and was trying to organize hunters to register truffle lands to protect the woodlands. Although truffles with their whopping price tags, have come to represent affluence, luxury, and culinary pyrotechnics, it's affecting to realize that experience starts with a man and his dog foraging in the woods at night.

CLAY-BAKED PORK ROAST WITH TRUFFLED LENTILS

I was seduced by clay pot cookery while visiting my friend Daphne Zepos at her family home on the Greek island of Siphnos. The people of this island are known for their chickpeas, which they cook in beehive-shaped clay pots. Every Saturday at dusk, neighbors all across the island meet at outdoor communal ovens. They catch up on a little gossip as the men stoke the ovens with mountain shrubs. The ovens are then packed, sealed, left to smolder throughout the night. The next day, after church, the women retrieve their pots for lunch. The flavors in those simple beans are absolutely astonishing.

In this recipe, the clay keeps the meat moist and traps the fragrance of the truffles. Most cooks will tell you to avoid cooking beans in wine, but combining these two ingredients for the long cooking time keeps the lentils from disintegrating. Bring the sealed clay pot to the table, and when you open it, your guests will be treated to an unforgettable aroma.

SERVES 4

2 tablespoons olive oil

1 bone-in 3-pound pork shoulder roast

Kosher salt to taste, plus 1 tablespoon

Freshly ground black pepper to taste

3 onions, cut in half

2 whole cloves

2 stalks celery with leaves, each cut in 3 pieces

3 carrots, peeled, cut each into 3 pieces

3 cloves garlic, smashed and peeled

2 cups dry red wine

¾ cup green French lentils (lentilles du Puy)

(continued on next page)

1 bay leaf

4 sprigs thyme

1½ cups water

1 fresh or frozen black winter truffle (about 1½ ounces)

2 tablespoons chopped fresh flat-leaf parsley

1. Soak the 2 halves of a medium clay pot in the sink with water to cover for 30 minutes and then drain. Preheat the oven to 350°F.

2. In a large skillet over medium-high heat, heat the olive oil. Season the roast with salt and pepper to taste and brown the meat on all sides. Set the roast aside on a plate. Stud an onion with the cloves. Add the vegetables and garlic to the pan and sauté over medium-high heat until lightly browned, 5 to 7 minutes. Using a slotted spoon, transfer the vegetables to the clay pot. Drain any excess fat from the pan. Pour the wine into the pan and cook over high heat, stirring to scrape up any browned bits from the bottom of the pan. Pour the wine into the clay pot.

3. Scatter the lentils, bay leaf, and thyme in the bottom of the clay pot. Add the 1 tablespoon kosher salt and pepper to taste. Place the pork roast in the pot and add the water. Cover the pot with its lid and place in the oven. Braise the meat until tender, about 3 hours, turning the roast every hour to make sure that it cooks evenly.

4. Chop the truffle and add it to the pot, stirring it into the lentils. Put the clay lid on the pot and return the pot to the oven. Turn the oven off and let the pot sit in the oven for about 20 minutes to allow the truffles to perfume the lentils and meat. Bring the clay pot to the table, remove the lid just before serving, and add the parsley. Slice the pork and serve with the lentils.

SQUAB WITH BLACK TRUFFLE AND FOIE GRAS

This is what I serve when I want to pull out all the stops to celebrate a landmark occasion. Squab, my favorite game bird, is both lean and rich-tasting, and a joy to cook. As with many game birds, the breast meat should be served rare while the legs should be fully cooked. Simmering the legs in the liquid destined for the sauce contributes a fuller game flavor to it. If boning the squabs is intimidating, ask your butcher to separate the breast and legs for you, but keep the bones for your sauce.

SERVES 4

4 squabs

3 tablespoons vegetable oil

3 cups brown chicken stock (page 172)

1 shallot, sliced

¾ cup dry red wine, such as Pinot Noir or Cabernet

½ bay leaf

2 whole cloves

2 sprigs thyme

1 sprig parsley

1½ teaspoons arrowroot dissolved in 1½ teaspoons water

2 tablespoons unsalted butter

½ to ¾ ounce fresh black winter truffle, or 1 ounce frozen truffle

½ teaspoon kosher salt to taste

Freshly ground black pepper to taste

Eight ½-inch slices baguette

3 ounces prepared or homemade foie gras mousse (page 59)

(continued on next page)

1. Remove the giblets from the inner cavity of the squabs and rinse the birds. Separate the livers from the other parts and use them in another recipe. Pat the birds dry with a paper towel. Use a boning knife to bone the squabs by cutting along the top of the breastbone and down along the ribcage to remove the breast in one piece. Separate the breast meat from the carcass at the wing joint and along the back. Bend the leg back out of its joint. Cut along the backbone to free the leg/thigh from the carcass. Repeat with the other side of the bird. Trim the skin so that it just covers the breast meat. Refrigerate the breast until 15 minutes before cooking. Chop the bones with a heavy knife or pull them into 2 to 3 pieces with your hands.

2. In a medium skillet over a medium heat, heat 1 tablespoon of the oil and, sauté the bones until browned, about 10 minutes. Add the chicken stock and simmer for 30 minutes, skimming any impurities that rise to the top. Strain the stock into a bowl or degreasing cup and remove any fat that may rise to the surface.

3. In a medium saucepan, combine the shallot, wine, bay leaf, cloves, thyme, and parsley. Bring to a simmer over medium heat and cook to reduce by half. Add the squab legs and stock. Set the pan slightly askew on the burner, so the impurities will drift to the cooler side of the pan, making it easier to skim them off. Braise the legs until tender, 30 minutes. Remove the legs from the liquid and set them aside. Strain the sauce into a medium saucepan. (The dish can be prepared up to this point 1 day ahead and refrigerated.)

4. Bring the sauce to a simmer over medium heat. Cook to reduce by about one-third or until thickened slightly. Whisk in the arrowroot mixture and bring to a boil to thicken. Lower heat and swirl in the butter. Slice the truffle paper-thin with a truffle slicer, mandoline, or very sharp knife and add to the sauce. Season the sauce with the salt and the pepper. Keep the sauce warm while you cook the squab.

5. To serve, toast the bread slices and spread the foie gras mousse on top. Preheat a large skillet and a small skillet over medium heat. Season the skin side of the breast with salt and pepper to taste. Add 1 tablespoon of the oil to each pan. Place the legs, skin-side down, in the smaller pan and cook until browned, about 5 minutes. Lay the breasts, skin-side down, in the large skillet and sauté over high heat for 3 to 5 minutes, or until a rich brown. Season the breast meat with salt and pepper to taste, turn, and cook for 2 to 3 minutes, or until firm to the touch with a bit of give, and rare inside. Transfer to a cutting board and let rest for 2 to 3 minutes before slicing.

6. To serve, place the foie gras croutons on a warm platter or divide among individual plates. Cut each breast into 5 slices, place them on top of each toast, and place the legs on the sides. Add any accumulated juices from the meat to the sauce. Nap each breast with the truffle sauce and serve immediately.

At the headquarters of Urbani Truffles, in Umbria, Italy, hunters sell their truffles bundled in simple blue and white cotton cloth. Believing that the cloths bring them luck for a successful hunt, some superstitious hunters will return days later to retrieve their special cloth. Throughout Italy, truffles are presented on these cloths or in woven willow baskets.

GRILLED PORTERHOUSE STEAK
WITH SUMMER TRUFFLE

This steak was the most popular cut in the eighteenth-century alehouses of London, hence the name porterhouse. *Those beer boys knew a good thing, for this cut is unsurpassed, with its large eye of the tenderloin, T-shaped bone, and succulent end of the loin. Food like this is the best of what home cooking can be: top-quality ingredients, cooked directly and simply, shared communally.*

SERVES 2 TO 4

One 2-pound aged prime porterhouse steak, about 2 inches thick

Coarse sea salt and freshly ground black pepper to taste

2 ounces fresh summer truffle

3 tablespoons top-quality extra-virgin olive oil

2 tablespoons water

1 medium shallot, minced (optional)

1. Remove the steak from the refrigerator 30 minutes before cooking. Prepare an outdoor grill or preheat the broiler. If cooking over a live fire, make 2 mounds of coals in the grill, one larger than the other. Heat the coals until white hot.

2. Dry the meat well and season one side with salt and pepper. If broiling, place the meat, seasoned-side up, on a rack over a pan. Place 2 to 4 inches from the heat source, depending on the potency of your broiler. Broil for about 7 minutes, or until charred brown. Turn and salt and pepper the other side. Broil for 3 to 5 minutes, or until an instant-read thermometer inserted in the steak registers 120°F for rare or 125°F for medium rare.

If cooking over live coals, start the meat over the hottest part of the large mound of fire. Season the meat on one side with salt and pepper and grill that side for 8 to 10 minutes, or until charred. Season the steak, turn, and cook the other side for 3 to 5 minutes. Transfer the steak to the smaller mound of coals and cook until an instant-read thermometer inserted in the steak registers 120°F for rare or 125°F for medium rare.

3. Meanwhile, slice the truffles paper-thin with a truffle slicer, a mandoline, or a very sharp knife. Place the truffle slices in a skillet large enough to accommodate the steak. When the meat has finished cooking, place it on top of the truffle slices and let it rest for at least 10 minutes, turning once.

4. Transfer the meat to a cutting board. Add the olive oil and water to the skillet and bring to a simmer. Season with salt and pepper to taste. Pour the heated truffles and juices over the steak. Slice the steak and serve the minced shallot on the side for guests to add, if desired.

Attempts to cultivate truffles in the United States have been mixed, with low production and truffles of poor aroma. A promising area for truffle farming is north Texas. According to Rosario Sarfina, president of Urbani, U.S.A, a truffle producer, "The hills of Texas are just like Provence." (Truffle cowboys?) Part of the truffle's charm is its unpredictability and wildness. Although it would be wonderful to find a way to sustain this product, I wonder if we would be as taken with them if we could buy truffles with the same ease as a bunch of bananas?

SAUTÉED MAGRET WITH
GINGER AND BLACK PEPPER FOIE GRAS SAUCE

"Duck is too fatty" is the usual litany. One remedy for this is slow roast-
ing, which renders the fat, crisps the skin, and thoroughly cooks the meat.
A magret, *the breast from a foie gras duck, is dry when prepared this*
way. This meat is better cooked on the rare side. Score the skin to open a
pathway for the fat to render, and cook the breast-skin side very slowly.

SERVES 2 TO 3

2 teaspoons, plus 3 tablespoons unsalted butter

1-inch piece of fresh ginger, peeled and chopped

1 shallot, chopped

½ teaspoon black peppercorns, cracked

1 bay leaf, crumbled

⅔ cup red port wine

2 cups brown chicken stock (page 172)

2 magret duck breasts

1 ounce fresh A-, B-, or C-grade duck foie gras (see page 41)

2 teaspoons arrowroot, dissolved in 2 teaspoons water

½ teaspoon kosher salt, plus salt to taste

Freshly ground black pepper to taste

⅛ teaspoon red wine vinegar

1. Melt the 2 teaspoons of butter in a medium saucepan. Add the ginger, shallot, peppercorns, and bay leaf. Cook over high heat, stirring
frequently, until browned, about 5 minutes. Remove the pan from
heat, add the port, and return to a boil. (The wine may flame briefly.)
Simmer the wine until the mixture looks jammy. Add the stock and
simmer to reduce by half. Set the pan slightly askew on the burner so
the impurities drift to the cooler side of the pan, making it easier to
skim them off. As the sauce reduces, skim any scum or impurities.

(continued on next page)

2. Meanwhile, prepare the duck breasts: Working with the breasts skin-side down, trim the surface of the meat of any sinew, excess fat, and tenderloin. (Toss any bits of meat into the sauce to boost the duck flavor.) Trim the skin so that it is the same size as the breast. Turn the breasts over. Using a sharp boning knife or paring knife, score the breast into a crosshatch pattern. Draw the knife across the skin, making parallel cuts through the skin and into the fat, no more than ¼ inch apart, running from one edge of the breast to the other. The cuts should be deep into the fat.

3. To finish the sauce, in a small food processor puree the foie gras with the 3 tablespoons butter. Whisk the arrowroot mixture into the sauce and bring the sauce to a boil. Reduce the heat and add the foie gras mixture, whisking constantly until it is absorbed into the sauce. Strain the sauce and season with the ½ teaspoon salt, pepper, and vinegar. Keep the sauce warm, but do not boil.

4. Set an empty can or metal bowl by the stove to pour the fat into as the breasts cook. Heat a large, heavy skillet over high heat. Lay the duck in the pan, skin-side down, and cook for 1 minute to start rendering the fat. Hold the breasts in the pan with tongs or your fingers and pour off all the fat. Reduce the heat to very low. Continue cooking, periodically pressing down on the breast and pouring off any fat in the pan. Cook the breast until the skin is crisp and the fat is rendered, about 15 minutes. Don't be tempted to speed up this process, or the skin will brown before the fat has completely rendered. The skin will shrink considerably and take on a mahogany color. When the skin is crisp, increase heat to high and season the breast meat with salt and pepper to taste. Turn the breast and sauté until rare to medium rare, about 2 minutes. Remove from heat and let rest, skin-side up, on a cutting board for 4 to 5 minutes.

5. Cut the breast into thin slices. Pour the sauce onto individual plates or a platter, fan the breast slices over it, and serve immediately.

MEDALLIONS OF BEEF WITH FOIE GRAS AND TRUFFLES

This winning combination is known in the classic French repertoire as tournedos Rossini. The story is that the composer Rossini, a devoted fan of truffles, asked a chef to prepare this dish. The chef balked, suggesting that it was ill-conceived. The maestro said that if the chef was offended, the maestro himself could prepare the dish quickly while the chef's back was turned. The word tournedos *thus supposedly comes from the French phrase* tourner le dos, *to turn one's back. Prepare this when you are pouring a prodigious red wine, and you surely won't be vexed.*

SERVES 4

SAUCE:

⅔ **cup Rainwater Madeira**

2 tablespoons minced shallot

1 sprig thyme

½ **bay leaf**

2 cups veal stock (page 173)

1½ **teaspoons arrowroot mixed with** 1½ **teaspoons water (optional)**

1 to 2 tablespoons cold unsalted butter

¾ **teaspoon kosher salt, plus salt to taste**

Freshly ground black pepper to taste

½ **teaspoon red wine vinegar**

½ **to 1 ounce fresh or preserved black winter truffle**

Four 4-ounce filet of beef (tenderloin) medallions, about 1½ **inches thick, at room temperature**

Kosher salt and freshly ground black pepper to taste

2 tablespoons vegetable oil

Four 1-ounce grade-A or -B duck foie gras medallions (see page 41)

(continued on next page)

1. To make the sauce: In a saucepan, combine the Madeira, shallot, thyme, and bay leaf. Bring to a gentle simmer and cook until the wine is reduced to a light syrup coating the shallots. (The wine may flame briefly.)

2. Pour the stock into the wine reduction and simmer until reduced by half. Skim off any impurities that rise to the surface. If the sauce is not thick enough to nap the meat, whisk the arrowroot mixture into the sauce and bring to a full boil to thicken. Lower heat and whisk in the butter. Season with the ¾ teaspoon salt, the pepper, and vinegar. Slice the truffle paper-thin with a truffle slicer, mandoline, or very sharp knife and add to the sauce. Set aside and keep warm in a double boiler over hot water for up to 1 hour. (You may need to adjust the consistency with a bit of water if the sauce thickens.)

3. Meanwhile, pat the beef medallions dry with paper towels and season one side of the meat with salt and pepper. Heat a heavy skillet over low heat. Add the oil to the pan, increase the heat to high, and place the meat, seasoned-side down, in the pan. Sauté until the steaks are a rich burnished brown on the bottom, about 4 minutes. Season the remaining side with salt and pepper to taste, turn, reduce the heat slightly, and brown the other side, 3 to 4 minutes. Brown the sides of the medallions by standing them on their sides. Transfer the meat to a plate while you sear the foie gras.

4. Wipe out the skillet and heat it over high heat. Season the foie gras medallions with salt and pepper to taste. Add the medallions to the pan and cook for 1 to 2 minutes, or until a deep brown on the bottom. Drain off any excess fat. Turn the foie gras with a metal spatula and cook for 30 seconds to 1 minute, or until the foie gras softens but still has some resilience. Transfer to paper towels to drain.

5. To serve, remove any strings from the medallions and place the medallions on warmed plates or a platter. Top with the foie gras and nap with the sauce, making sure that a couple of slices of truffles rest on each serving of foie gras. Serve immediately.

WHOLE ROASTED FOIE GRAS WITH WINTER VEGETABLES

If a foie gras dish can be rustic, this one is. A whole liver is seared and oven-roasted on a bed of cabbage and vegetables, similar to the Alsatian baekeoffe, *a preparation of foie gras baked under a pastry lid. Foie gras has different qualities, depending on how you cook it. Seared foie gras is moltenly rich, while a slow-cooked terrine is satiny, smooth, and buttery; surprisingly, roasting brings out, in a pleasant way, the liver taste, and tempers the richness.*

In Jewish culinary traditions, foie gras and goose fat are kosher. While working on recipes for this book, I was invited to a friend's Passover seder and brought this dish, which was thoroughly appreciated. Serve this with boiled small red potatoes to absorb the delicious broth.

SERVES 6 TO 8

1 grade-A foie gras (about 1¼ pounds), preferably Canadian

½ head savoy cabbage, cored and shredded (about 12 ounces)

Kosher salt and freshly ground black pepper to taste

4 carrots, peeled and sliced

2 leeks, including light green parts, sliced and rinsed

1 turnip, peeled and cut into large dice

1 cup dry white wine

5 allspice berries

⅓ cup golden raisins

1½ cups chicken stock (page 173)

2 tablespoons chopped fresh flat-leaf parsley

1. Remove the foie gras from the refrigerator 1 hour before preparing. Separate the larger lobe from the smaller one by gently pulling them apart. Place the smooth side of the foie gras on a work surface. Find the spot in the larger lobe where the veins surface. With a small paring knife, pry the foie gras open and follow the major veins into the liver. (The veins form tributaries from a central main core. Remove

the veins from the liver by pulling gently, using pliers if needed.) Take care not to break up the liver too much. Re-form the liver into a compact shape. Repeat with the smaller lobe. Cover and refrigerate until firm, about 1 hour.

2. Preheat the oven to 350°F. In a medium saucepan of salted boiling water, cook the cabbage for 4 to 5 minutes, or until bright green and wilted. Drain.

3. Heat a cast-iron Dutch oven or heavy flameproof casserole over medium heat. Season the foie gras with salt and pepper to taste. Increase heat to high and brown the two lobes on all sides over high heat, which takes about 5 minutes. The goal is to sear the liver without cooking it through. Transfer the liver to a plate. Sauté the carrots, leeks, and turnip in the drippings with a pinch of salt for 5 minutes. Add the wine, allspice, and raisins. Simmer for about 5 minutes. Add the stock, cover, and simmer for 5 to 7 minutes. Add the cabbage, season with salt and pepper to taste, and simmer for 5 minutes, or until the vegetables are tender.

4. Place the 2 lobes together in the center of the cabbage and roast in the oven for 20 to 30 minutes, or until an instant-read thermometer inserted in the center of the foie gras registers between 115° and 120°F.

5. Transfer the vegetables and cooking liquid to a large rimmed platter or divide among warmed plates. Slice the liver and place on top of the vegetables. Sprinkle with parsley and serve.

SIDE DISHES

Although we generally like to make the most of luxurious ingredients as the center of our meals, they can also add a little finesse to the dishes that sit to the side of the plate. This handful of recipes shows how truffle oil or foie gras renderings add a dimension of flavor that will make even the simplest dish special.

❦

Leeks with Black Truffle Vinaigrette

Truffled Celery Root Mashed Potatoes

Mixed Greens with Foie Gras Renderings

*Mushroom and Haricot Vert Salad with
Black-Truffled Vinaigrette*

Truffle-Glazed Parsnips with Onions and Chestnuts

Warm Summer-Truffled Potato Salad

LEEKS WITH BLACK TRUFFLE VINAIGRETTE

A black truffle vinaigrette gives a lavish finish to this comforting French bistro standard. Covering the braising leeks with a piece of parchment paper keeps them moist and concentrates the cooking juices. This is an ideal accompaniment to a crisp roast chicken or sautéed fish.

SERVES 6

9 leeks, including light green parts

½ cup extra-virgin olive oil

1 cup water

1 teaspoon kosher salt, plus to taste

Freshly ground black pepper to taste

½ teaspoon minced fresh thyme

2 tablespoons white wine vinegar

2 tablespoons Dijon mustard

5 tablespoons black truffle oil

2 tablespoons chopped preserved black truffles with juice

1. Trim the long roots from the leeks, but leave the root base intact so the layers of the leek remain together. Cut each leek in half lengthwise. Rinse the leeks under running water, pulling the layers open to flush out the grit. Soak the leeks in a large bowl of cold water to clean.

2. In a large skillet, lay the leeks in a single layer. Add the olive oil and water and season with the 1 teaspoon salt and the pepper. Bring the liquid to a boil, then reduce heat to a simmer. Cover the leeks with a piece of parchment paper cut into a circle the size of the pan. Braise the leeks for 15 minutes. Check for doneness and, using tongs, transfer any of the leeks that are easily pierced with a fork to a platter. (Keep the leeks in long, intact pieces.) Replace the parchment lid

and cook the remaining leeks until tender but not mushy, about 5 more minutes. Transfer the remaining leeks to the platter and arrange them neatly, cut-side down. Reserve the braising liquid.

3. Bring the braising liquid to a boil and cook to reduce until slightly thickened. You should have about ⅔ cup liquid. Pour the liquid into a medium bowl. Stir in the thyme, vinegar, and mustard. Gradually whisk in the truffle oil to make an emulsified dressing. Add the truffle pieces with their juice. Add salt and pepper to taste. Pour the dressing over the leeks. Serve now, or let sit for up to 2 hours at room temperature.

A Piedmont *trifalau* told me — as he freed a truffle from the ground — that hunting used to be better. The modern prosperity of the region has changed the woods. The peasants used to collect the loose underbrush to heat their homes, which kept the forest floor drier—a far better environment for truffles.

TRUFFLED CELERY ROOT MASHED POTATOES

Truffles and mashed potatoes are a modern American classic. The addition of celery root to the mix brings another dimension to this combination.

SERVES 4

1 pound russet (baking) potatoes, peeled and quartered

1 large celery root, peeled and cubed

2 teaspoons kosher salt

¾ cup half-and-half

2 tablespoons prepared or homemade truffle butter (page 175)

Freshly ground white pepper to taste

1. In a medium saucepan, combine the potatoes and celery root. Add water to cover and 1 teaspoon of the salt. Bring to a boil, reduce the heat to a simmer, and cook until completely tender, about 25 minutes. Drain. Puree the vegetables in a food mill or with an immersion blender until light and smooth. (Don't use a ricer, or the puree will be too coarse.) Return to the pan and keep warm.

2. In a small saucepan, heat the half-and-half to just scalding. Remove from heat, add the truffle butter, and stir until melted. Whisk the liquid into the potatoes over medium heat. Add the remaining 1 teaspoon salt and the pepper and serve.

MIXED GREENS WITH FOIE GRAS RENDERINGS

When making a terrine of foie gras there is always a surplus of delicious fat left over, which I use for roasting potatoes, frying eggs, and even sautéing fish. But one of my favorite uses for it is with greens. You need to buy what seems like enough greens to feed a small army, as a mountain of them cooks down to a couple of handfuls. I like peppery mustard greens mixed with pungent broccoli rabe and balanced with flavorful escarole or Swiss chard. Trim away the green's tougher stems and tear the leaves into manageable pieces before rinsing them in a large bowl of cold water.

SERVES 4

3 tablespoons rendered foie gras fat

**1½ pounds mixed greens, such as broccoli rabe, escarole, mustard
    greens, or Swiss chard, stemmed and torn into pieces
    (about 16 cups)**

¼ teaspoon kosher salt

Freshly ground black pepper to taste

⅓ cup water

In a large soup pot, heat the foie gras fat over medium heat. Add the greens, salt, and pepper. Increase the heat to high and cook the greens, stirring frequently, until they begin to wilt. Add the water, cover, and cook for 5 to 7 minutes, or until the greens are softened and the broccoli rabe florets are crisp-tender. Drain the excess liquid. Serve hot or at room temperature.

MUSHROOM AND HARICOT VERT SALAD WITH
BLACK-TRUFFLED VINAIGRETTE

This recipe was part of a Christmas buffet article I wrote for Fine
Cooking *magazine. It's a great dish to do ahead for large groups and
is an excellent accent to filet of beef or other festive roasts.*

SERVES 4 TO 6

VINAIGRETTE:

1½ teaspoons Dijon mustard

1½ tablespoons white wine vinegar

1½ teaspoons minced fresh thyme

½ teaspoon kosher salt

Freshly ground black pepper to taste

6 tablespoons black truffle olive oil

12 ounces haricots verts or tender green beans, trimmed

12 ounces cremini mushrooms, thinly sliced

2 tablespoons minced shallot

1 small endive (preferably red)

1. To make the vinaigrette: In a small bowl, whisk the mustard,
vinegar, thyme, salt, and pepper together. Gradually whisk the truffle
oil into the vinegar to make an emulsified sauce. Set aside.

2. In a large pot of salted boiling water, cook the beans until crisp-
tender, 2 to 3 minutes. Drain and plunge the beans into ice water to
stop the cooking and set their color. Drain and pat dry.

3. To serve, toss the beans, mushrooms, shallot, and vinaigrette
together in a bowl. Remove 3 or 4 of the outer leaves of the endive.
Cut them into diagonal slices and add to the salad. Line salad plates
with the remaining endive leaves and place the salad in the center.

TRUFFLE-GLAZED PARSNIPS WITH ONIONS AND CHESTNUTS

Eating foods in their true season is a tenet of any great cook. The winter months, however, can be a challenge for even the best cooks when the vegetable larder is a little bare. But when the aroma of chestnuts fills my kitchen, I am reminded of the wisdom of eating seasonally. The flavor, texture, and romance of chestnuts is the ideal counter to the winter-food doldrums.

All that being said, once you start peeling the chestnut's tough shell the love affair can be a short one. Cutting a small X in the flat side of the nuts and either roasting or boiling them speeds the chore. Buy extra nuts, because there are always a couple that don't pass muster when peeled. The combination of parsnips, onions, and chestnuts, finished off with a light swirl of truffle butter, is outstanding with venison or other game meats.

SERVES 6

8 ounces chestnuts (see note)

12 ounces pearl onions (3 cups)

4 teaspoons unsalted butter

1 cup chicken stock (page 173)

1 teaspoon minced fresh thyme

½ teaspoon kosher salt

Freshly ground black pepper to taste

1 pound parsnips, diced

2 tablespoons truffle butter (page 175)

1 tablespoon minced fresh flat-leaf parsley

1. Cut an X in the flat side of the chestnuts. Put the chestnuts in a medium saucepan and add water to cover by 2 inches. Bring to a boil and cook for 5 to 7 minutes. Using a slotted spoon, remove the nuts from the water. Peel off the shell and the dark inner skin. (It is easier to peel chestnuts if you keep them warm. Return them to the water if they become difficult to peel.)

2. To peel the pearl onions, trim the root end and make an X in the root with a paring knife. Cook in a saucepan of boiling water for 5 minutes. Drain and plunge into a bowl of cold water. Drain and gently press the onions to pop them from their skins.

3. In a large skillet or Dutch oven over medium heat, melt the unsalted butter. Add the onions and chestnuts and cook, stirring occasionally, for 5 to 7 minutes, or until lightly browned. Add the stock, thyme, salt, and pepper. Cut a circle of parchment to fit just inside the pan. Cover the onion mixture with the paper and cook over medium-low heat for 10 to 15 minutes, or until the onions are just tender.

4. Add the diced parsnips, re-cover, and cook for 7 to 10 more minutes, or until the parsnips are tender but firm. There should be enough liquid to coat and glaze the vegetables evenly. If not, add 2 tablespoons of water. Add the truffle butter and swirl to glaze the vegetables. Taste and adjust the seasoning. Add the parsley and serve.

Note: If you can't find fresh chestnuts, don't be tempted by jarred or canned ones, for they are really unsatisfactory. Instead, look for dried chestnuts at a specialty market. Before using in this recipe, they should be hydrated in simmering water for 10 to 15 minutes.

WARM SUMMER-TRUFFLED POTATO SALAD

Try this salad with pan-seared sea scallops as a great way to enjoy "surf and turf."

SERVES 4

1 tablespoon extra-virgin olive oil

2 ounces pancetta, trimmed of excess fat and diced

1¼ pounds red-skinned potatoes, cut into ¼-inch slices

1 cup dry white wine

2 cups water

2 teaspoons kosher salt

1 bay leaf

1 large sprig thyme

VINAIGRETTE:

1 tablespoon white wine vinegar

1 tablespoon minced shallot

½ teaspoon minced garlic

1 teaspoon minced fresh thyme

½ teaspoon kosher salt, plus salt to taste

Freshly ground black pepper to taste

3 tablespoons black truffle oil

¾ to 1 ounce preserved sliced summer truffle, with juice

8 to 10 flat-leaf parsley leaves

1. In a small skillet over medium heat, heat the olive oil and sauté the pancetta for about 3 minutes, or until it has firmed and rendered a bit of fat. Using a slotted spoon, transfer the pancetta to paper towels to drain.

2. In a medium saucepan, combine the potatoes, wine, water, salt, bay leaf, and thyme. Bring to a boil, reduce heat to a simmer, and simmer the potatoes until tender but not mushy, about 4 minutes. Drain and place in a medium bowl.

3. Meanwhile, make the vinaigrette: In a small bowl, whisk the vinegar, shallot, garlic, thyme, the ½ teaspoon salt, and pepper together. Gradually whisk in the truffle oil to make an emulsified dressing.

4. Toss the warm potatoes with the vinaigrette, pancetta, truffle slices, and juice. Season with salt and pepper. Transfer salad to a serving dish, scatter the parsley leaves on top, and serve.

PANTRY

BROWN CHICKEN STOCK

MAKES ABOUT 4 QUARTS

6 pounds chicken necks, backs, and bones

2 onions, halved

4 carrots, quartered

4 stalks celery, quartered

Dark-green tops of 1 leek

1 tomato, chopped

3 cloves garlic

2 bay leaves

2 sprigs thyme, or 1 teaspoon dried thyme

¼ cup parsley stems

1 cup water, plus 5 quarts

1. Preheat the oven to 400°F. Spread the chicken parts and bones out in a large roasting pan. Roast for 1½ to 2 hours, or until golden brown, turning periodically to assure even cooking.

2. With a large spoon, skim about 3 tablespoons chicken fat from the roasting pan. Add to an 8- to 10-quart stockpot. Sauté the vegetables, garlic, and herbs in the stockpot over high heat until browned, about 10 minutes.

3. Add the bones to the stockpot and discard the excess fat. Add the 1 cup water to the roasting pan and stir over medium heat to scrape up any browned bits from the pan. Add this liquid to the stockpot along with the remaining 5 quarts water. Bring to a boil and skim off the fat and the scum. Reduce heat to low and simmer, uncovered, for 4 to 6 hours. Skim occasionally. Strain and let cool. Refrigerate for up to 3 days or freeze for up to 3 months. Remove any fat that congeals on the top before using.

CHICKEN STOCK

MAKES ABOUT 4 QUARTS

6 pounds chicken backs, necks, and bones

5 quarts water

3 onions, halved

3 carrots, quartered

3 stalks celery, quartered

1 bay leaf

1 large sprig thyme

Handful of flat-leaf parsley stems

Combine all the ingredients in an 8-quart stockpot. Bring just to a boil and skim off the fat and scum. Reduce heat to very low and simmer, uncovered, for 4 to 6 hours, skimming occasionally. Strain and let cool. Cover and refrigerate for up to 3 days or freeze for up to 3 months. Remove any fat that rises to the top before using.

VEAL STOCK

I learned this somewhat unconventional method for making stock—roasting the vegetables but not the bones—from Michael Romano, the chef of the award-winning Union Square Cafe. It produces a beautiful top-quality stock without the funky bitterness that some browned stocks can have. Many home cooks may not feel they want to bother to make veal stock, because it takes so long. But the rewards are high, for there is no substitute for a well-made stock. Having a couple of containers in the freezer for sauces and stews will boost your culinary efforts enormously.

(continued on next page)

5 pounds veal bones

5 quarts water

1 pound beef shin

2 carrots, coarsely chopped

3 unpeeled onions, quartered

2 stalks celery, coarsely chopped

2 cups chopped leek greens, rinsed

1 head garlic, halved horizontally

2 tablespoons vegetable oil

3 tablespoons tomato paste

1 teaspoon dried thyme

1 bay leaf

6 sprigs flat-leaf parsley

1. Preheat the oven to 450°F. Rinse the bones in cold water until the water runs clear. Place the bones in a stockpot with all but 1 cup of the water. Bring to a boil, skim off the foam, and reduce heat to a very gentle simmer.

2. In a roasting pan, combine the beef shin and vegetables. Coat with the oil and the tomato paste. Roast in the oven for 45 minutes to 1 hour, or until a deep, rich brown.

3. Add the meat and vegetables to the stockpot along with the thyme, bay leaf, and parsley. Add the remaining 1 cup water to the roasting pan and stir over medium heat to scrape up any browned bits from the bottom of the pan. Add this liquid to the stockpot. (Add water if needed to cover the vegetables.) Reduce heat to low and cook at a bare simmer, uncovered, for 10 hours. It is important not to boil the stock, or it will cloud. You know you have set the heat just right when a bubble or two breaks the surface of the water about once a minute.

4. Strain and let cool to room temperature. Cover and refrigerate for up to 3 days or freeze for up to 3 months. Remove any fat that has risen to the top before using.

TRUFFLE OIL

There are many truffle oils on the market, some with good truffle fla-
voring and others that could double as gasoline. If you have enough
truffles, make your own oil, you will be rewarded with authentic flavor.

½ cup mild extra-virgin olive oil, mild seed oil, or a combination

¼ to ½ ounce white or black truffle, preferably fresh, thinly sliced

Pinch of kosher salt

If using a white truffle, combine the oil, truffle, and salt in a small
bowl. Stir lightly to dissolve the salt. Cover with plastic wrap and set
aside at room temperature for at least 1 hour or up to 6 hours. If you
use a black truffle, warm the oil ever so gently, then add the truffle
and set aside for 2 hours. Taste the oil after a couple hours; it should
have a nice truffle flavor and aroma. Store the oil in an airtight container in the refrigerator and use within 2 days.

TRUFFLE BUTTER

To flavor butter with white truffles, simply store the two together in a
sealed container. With black truffles, make truffle butter, to stretch the
flavor of the truffle to another day.

½ cup (1 stick) unsalted butter at room temperature

¼ to 1 ounce whole, pieces, or peelings of fresh or frozen black winter
  truffle, minced

⅛ teaspoon kosher salt

In a medium bowl, work the butter with a wooden spoon until it is
creamy and light. Add the truffle to the butter. Season with salt. Lay
a sheet of plastic wrap about 10 inches long on the work surface.
Transfer the butter to the center of the plastic wrap. Roll the butter up
in the plastic to make a log. Twist the ends of the plastic like a party
favor. Refrigerate for up to 2 days or freeze for up to 3 months.

Urbani U.S.A.
29–24 40th Avenue
Long Island City, NY 11101
www.urbani.com
Truffles, caviar, and foie gras.

Urbani West
5851 West Washington
Boulevard
Culver City, CA 90232
www.urbani.com
Truffles, caviar, and foie gras.

Boscovivo
107 East 31st Street
New York, NY 10016
877-TARTUFO
www.boscovivo.com
Truffles and truffle products.

D'Artagnan
280 Wilson Avenue
Newark, NJ 07105
800-D'Artagnan
www.dartagnan.com
*Domestic and imported foie
gras and truffles.*

Hudson Valley Foie Gras
80 Brooks Road
Ferndale, NY 12734
877-Buy-Foie
Domestic foie gras.

Petrossian
419 West 13th Street
New York, NY 10014
1-800-828-9241
*Fine Russian caviars and
imported foie gras.*

Browne Trading Company
Merril's Wharf
260 Commercial Street
Portland, ME 04101
800-944-7848
www.Browne-Trading.com
*Iranian, Russian, and American
caviars.*

Tsar Nicoulai Caviar
144 King Street
San Francisco, CA 94107
800-952-2842
www.tsarnicoulai.com
American and Russian caviars.

INDEX

TABLE OF EQUIVALENTS

LIQUID AND DRY MEASURES

The exact equivalents in the following tables have been rounded for convenience.

U.S.	Metric
¼ teaspoon	1.25 milliliters
½ teaspoon	2.5 milliliters
1 teaspoon	5 milliliters
1 tablespoon (3 teaspoons)	15 milliliters
1 fluid ounce (2 tablespoons)	30 milliliters
¼ cup	60 milliliters
⅓ cup	80 milliliters
1 cup	240 milliliters
1 pint (2 cups)	480 milliliters
1 quart (4 cups, 32 ounces)	960 milliliters
1 gallon (4 quarts)	3.84 liters
1 ounce (by weight)	28 grams
1 pound	454 grams
2.2 pounds	1 kilogram

OVEN TEMPERATURES

Fahrenheit	Celsius	Gas
250	120	½
275	140	1
300	150	2
325	160	3
350	180	4
375	190	5
400	200	6
425	220	7
450	230	8
475	240	9
500	260	10

LENGTH MEASURES

U.S.	Metric
⅛ inch	3 millimeters
¼ inch	6 millimeters
½ inch	12 millimeters
1 inch	2.5 centimeters